VIEWING THE LIFELESS BODY

A Coroner and his Inquests held in Nottinghamshire Public Houses during the Nineteenth Century

1828 to 1866

by

Bernard V. Heathcote

Bernard Heathcote is now retired from full-time work. He was Medical Information & Services Manager in the Research Department of The Boots Company PLC. His extra-mural interest has for many years been focused upon aspects of the history of photography, both at a national and a local level. An interest he shares with his wife, Pauline, and together they have published numerous papers on the subject and are the authors of three books. This current publication departs from his traditional activities and stems from ongoing studies on the history of the village public house in Nottinghamshire, this work alerted him to the fact that at one time coroner's inquests routinely took place on licensed premises.

Foreword

What an amazing book! It is a "*must read*" for historians and is a wonderful insight into our past, particularly the different functions of our public houses. How many people sat having a meal consider the past use of the same room? How things have changed! My office now deals with 6800 deaths in a year with 500 inquests. The Coroner's Office in Nottinghamshire now costs over one million pounds a year.

Fortunately, juries no longer have to see the body but sadly I cannot hold inquests in public houses.

The verdicts have not changed greatly, but medicine has advanced tremendously and so have the causes of death. I could not accept a death of fright or excessive eating.

The book covers the career of Christopher Swann in fascinating detail and discusses not only his work, but also Mr. Swann's resistance to the justices to reduce his costs. Some things never change!

It has been a great honour for me to write the foreword to this book. I applaud and am in great admiration of Bernard Heathcote as there has been an exceptionally large amount of research and time given to its creation.

The book is well written as it covers the complex work of Mr. Swann and is fully absorbing so you are unable to put it down until finished.

It will be widely read and enjoyed by all.

Dr. Nigel D. Chapman
H. M. Coroner for Nottinghamshire

Dedication

This book is dedicated to
the author's wife
PAULINE FLORENCE HEATHCOTE
as a small token of appreciation
for her loving support over many years.

CONTENTS

ELECTION OF
CORONER.

I take the earliest opportunity of informing the Freeholders of the County, that the

Election for a Coroner
IS OVER,

and that I have been elected to fill that Office by a MAJORITY of 293 Votes. I return my best Thanks to every Individual who has given me his Support, and I am happy to say that further exertions are unnecessary.

Christopher Swann.

STATE OF THE POLL.

SWANN, - - - - - - - -	732
SHILTON, - - - - - - -	439
MAJORITY, - -	293

Broadside issued by Christopher Swann announcing that he has been elected to serve as one of the two coroners for the County of Nottingham (May 1828)

The Coroner frequents more public-houses than any man alive. The smell of sawdust, beer, tobacco-smoke and spirits is inseparable in his vocation from death in its most awful shapes.

Charles Dickens: Bleak House, Chapter XI.

This book is the result of several years of research into the career of Christopher Swann who was one of the County Coroners for Nottinghamshire. His family was a very old and respectable one, members of which had for many years, filled public offices within the Borough of Nottingham. Swann was born on the 28th February 1793 in Nottingham, the third son of Edward and Mary Swann and baptised at Castle Gate Independent Chapel. His father was an Alderman, Justice of the Peace and elected to the office of Sheriff in the town in 1784 and its Mayor in 1805 and again in 1812.

When he was a young man Christopher Swann entered the legal profession, articled as a solicitor to Henry Enfield, at one time the Town Clerk and a Borough Coroner. On the death of Thomas Wright, one of the Coroners for the County of Nottingham, Swann offered himself as a candidate for this vacancy. He was subsequently elected in May 1828 and held the position for over 38 years until his death at the age of 73 on the 24th December 1866.

Throughout Swann's career most inquests were held on licensed premises and (as intimated by Charles Dickens - Bleak House 1852-53), he would have spent much of his time in public houses or travelling to and from them. The verdicts of the juries ranged from '*wilful murder*' to the conclusion that death came about entirely from '*natural causes*' or stating the oft-used terminology of the day '*by the sudden visitation of God*'. A selected number of these verdicts are discussed and the situations that led to the unnatural death of some of our Nottinghamshire folk are highlighted in Section III of this book. One must take note that Swann, in this period of our history, did not have the advantage of twenty-first century medical, pathological or forensic facilities and that the outcome of some of his inquests may seem at times somewhat strange to us. As a coroner he was constantly harangued, by the justices in the Quarter Sessions, to curtail the number of inquests he was taking, for the sole purpose of saving money from the county rate. To the credit of Swann, he stubbornly resisted the will of the judiciary, for he believed that it was all too easy to avoid the detection of a felonious killing, if an inquest were to be denied.

In order to qualify for the position of coroner it was conditional that the applicant should be a landowner, so that we may assume that he was a person with some social standing within the community. However, for some as yet unknown and inexplicable reason, Christopher Swann died in straitened circumstances and was heavily in debt.

Swann married Elizabeth Lois Marriott in the Nottinghamshire parish of Hawksworth; the ceremony taking place on the 20th June 1826. They had ten children (page 95) and of the eight that survived into adulthood, some entered the legal profession. One of his sons, Henry Kirke, occasionally assisted his father as his deputy during the latter years of his career.

I. THE CORONER'S OFFICE

Although the office of coroner is undoubtedly a very ancient one, it is safer to say that its date of birth is unknown and lost in the mists of antiquity. The earliest date conceded by historians is 1194, in this year the '*Articles of Eyre*' were issued which provided for three knights and one clerk to keep the pleas of the crown in each county. These elected individuals soon became known as coroners.

It appears that the primary object of the mediæval coroner was to keep watch over the profits of the Crown. His duties included making inquiries into treasure-trove, shipwrecks and to secure them for the King's profit. An inquest in cases of sudden death had a similar purpose, to see that the Crown was not deprived of its emoluments arising from the forfeiture of the goods and chattels of felons and outlaws. In those early years this appeared to have taken precedence over inquiring into the reason for death or even bringing the felon to justice.

These were the primary functions of the coroner in '*days of old*' but during the ensuing centuries they have been gradually limited to an enquiry upon '*the dead body of a person lying within his jurisdiction*'. His duty being to determine how, when, where and by what means the death occurred where there was reasonable doubt to suspect that such a person had suffered either a violent or unnatural death or died suddenly due to an unknown cause or had died in prison. He was also empowered to enquire into treasure-trove. There are a number of statutes that control the activities of the coroner and these various Acts are listed in Table 1. However, for the purpose of the current document only those that affect the office of Coroner Swann need be considered relevant i.e. prior to 1867. It is therefore not necessary to discuss the rôle of the late Victorian, or subsequent coroners but a number of books or articles are available[1-4] for additional and detailed information.

1. Election of a coroner to the vacant position in Nottinghamshire

Thomas Wright of Beeston was one of the Nottinghamshire Coroners from the 26th December 1805 until shortly before his death at the age of 81 on the 17th March 1828. Although the other County Coroner, Philip Richard Falkner or one of the Borough Coroners, would then have carried out Wright's duties on an interim basis it was a matter of urgency to appoint a replacement. Initially there were three contenders, John Ashwell of Epperstone, Christopher Swann of Nottingham and Caractacus D'Aubigny Shilton of Sneinton although Ashwell soon withdrew his application.

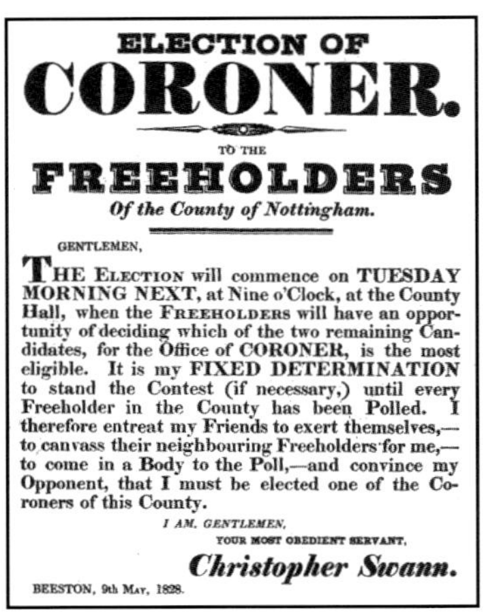
ELECTION OF

CORONER.

TO THE

FREEHOLDERS

Of the County of Nottingham.

GENTLEMEN,

THE ELECTION will commence on TUESDAY MORNING NEXT, at Nine o'Clock, at the County Hall, when the FREEHOLDERS will have an opportunity of deciding which of the two remaining Candidates, for the Office of CORONER, is the most eligible. It is my FIXED DETERMINATION to stand the Contest (if necessary,) until every Freeholder in the County has been Polled. I therefore entreat my Friends to exert themselves,—to canvass their neighbouring Freeholders for me,—to come in a Body to the Poll,—and convince my Opponent, that I must be elected one of the Coroners of this County.

I AM, GENTLEMEN,

YOUR MOST OBEDIENT SERVANT,

Christopher Swann.

BEESTON, 9th MAY, 1828.

Broadside issued by Christopher Swann announcing that the election for the coroner will commence on Tuesday 13th May 1828

Because there were still two candidates it was therefore necessary to hold an election for Wright's replacement. The Sheriff, John Emmerton Wescomb, announced that this was to be held at the Shire Hall on Tuesday 13th May 1828. The electorate was by tradition the attending freeholders of the county and excluded, of course, the ragbag

Table 1.

A selection of the Acts of Parliament relating to coroner's inquests

Date	Reference	Description
1275	3 Edw. I c.10	What sort of men shall be coroners
1276	4 Edw. I stat.2	Of what things a coroner shall inquire
1340	14 Edw. III c.8	No coroner be chosen unless he have land in fee sufficient in the same county, whereof he may answer to all manner of people
1354	28 Edw. III c.6	Who shall be coroners, and by whom and where they shall be chosen
1487	3 Hen. VII c.1	A coroner's duty after a murder has been committed
1509	1 Hen. VIII c.7	Coroner's fees
1752	25 Geo. II c.29	For giving a proper reward to coroners for the due execution of their office; and for the amoval of coroners upon a lawful conviction for certain misdemeanors
1818	58 Geo. III c.95	To regulate the election of coroners for counties
1823	4 Geo. IV c.52	To alter and amend the law relating to the interment of the remains of any person found felo-de-se
1825	6 Geo. IV c.50	For consolidating and amending the laws relative to jurors and juries
1836	6 & 7 Will. IV c.89	To provide for the attendance and remuneration of medical witnesses at coroner's inquests
1837	7 Will. IV & 1 Vict. c.68	To provide for payment of the expenses of holding coroner's inquests
1843	6 & 7 Vict. c.12	The more convenient holding of coroner's inquests
1844	7 & 8 Vict. c.92	To amend the law respecting the office of County Coroners
1846	9 & 10 Vict. c.62	To abolish deodands
1860	23 & 24 Vict. c.116	To amend the law relating to the election, duties, and payment of County Coroners
1870	33 & 34 Vict. c.77	To amend the laws relating to the qualifications, summoning, attendance, and remuneration of special and common juries
1882	45 & 46 Vict. c.19	To amend the law relating to the interment of any person found felo-de-se
1882	45 & 46 Vict. c.171-4	Appointment of Borough Coroners
1887	50 & 51 Vict. c.71	To consolidate the law relating to coroners
1892	55 & 56 Vict. c.56	To amend the law in relation to the appointment of coroners and deputy coroners in counties and boroughs
1902	2 Edw. VII c.28 s.21	From and after the 31st day of March 1907 no coroner's inquest shall be held in premises licensed for the sale of intoxicating liquors, or in any room, whether licensed or not, in any building licensed for the sale of intoxicating liquor, where other suitable premises have been provided for such inquest
1926	16 & 17 Geo. V c.59	To amend the law relating to coroners

category of women, children, lunatics and idiots. As was customary at the time, each candidate inserted publicity notices in the local press and also had broadsides printed for distribution.

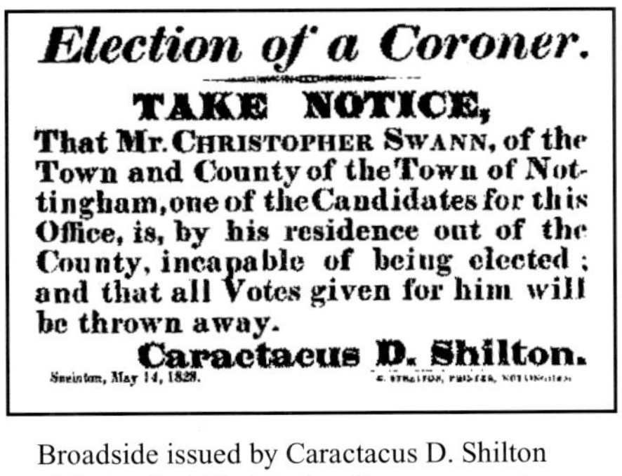
Election of a Coroner.

TAKE NOTICE,

That Mr. CHRISTOPHER SWANN, of the Town and County of the Town of Nottingham, one of the Candidates for this Office, is, by his residence out of the County, incapable of being elected; and that all Votes given for him will be thrown away.

Caractacus D. Shilton.

Broadside issued by Caractacus D. Shilton claiming that Christopher Swann was not eligible to be elected as a County Coroner

On the appointed day it proved to be an acrimonious meeting for Shilton objected to Swann's qualification on the grounds that he did not legally reside in Beeston, as he contended, but in the Borough of Nottingham and therefore should be eliminated from the contest. However, this objection whilst noted by the Under Sheriff was not accepted.[5] At a later date the Lord Chancellor rejected a petition by Shilton that Swann was not legally entitled to hold the office. His Lordship said that although Swann lived in the Borough of Nottingham he additionally owned land and property in the county and indeed held a tenancy for himself in Beeston. In addition, if only candidates residing in the county were to be considered, then it would deprive the electorate of qualified persons who were more likely to reside and work in the borough.[6] A second objection to Swann was that a number of his supporters came from the Borough of East Retford, which was if it so wished entitled to appoint its own coroner. Likewise, this was also over-ruled for the reason that the freeholders of this place contributed towards the county rate and therefore to the County Coroner's emolument and so it would be unjust to deprive them of a vote.

At an initial show of hands the result was somewhat inconclusive and a more organised election was scheduled for the following Thursday the 15th May 1828. At this meeting of the freeholders Christopher Swann was elected as one of the two coroners for the County of Nottingham by a majority of 293 votes, polling 732 against 439 for Mr. Shilton. He therefore joined Philip Richard Falkner; both appointments were, at that date, for the whole of the county. Although, traditionally there was an unwritten agreement that one would have a district which included parishes in the north of the county whilst the jurisdiction of the other, the current vacancy, was for those in the southern-most places.

This state of affairs continued until 1858 when the county was sub-divided, under the provision of an earlier Act of Parliament (7 & 8 Vict. c.92), into three distinct districts and a third coroner was appointed. The reason for this change was that the County of Nottingham was too large to be served by only two coroners as the travelling expenses of holding inquests were considerably larger than would be the case if the county were divided into smaller districts. The parishes encompassed by the District of Christopher Swann are enumerated in Table 2.

Table 2.

The parishes and places in the Nottingham District (assigned to Christopher Swann from 1858)

Adbolton	Costock	Langar-cum-Barnston	Standard Hill (Nottm.)
Annesley	Cotgrave	Lenton	Stanford
Arnold	Cropwell Bishop	Linby	Stanton-on-the-Wolds
Barton-in-Fabis	Cropwell Butler	Lindhurst	Stapleford
Basford	East Leake	Lowdham	Stoke Bardolph
Bassingfield	Eastwood	Mansfield	Strelley
Beeston	Edwalton	Mansfield Woodhouse	Sutton Bonington
Bilborough	Felley	Newstead	Sutton-in-Ashfield
Blidworth	Fulwood	Newton	Teversall
Bradmore	Gamston	Normanton-on-Soar	Thorpe-in-Glebis
Bramcote	Gedling	Normanton-on-the-Wolds	Thrumpton
Brewhouse Yard (Nottm.)	Gotham	Nuthall	Tithby
Broughton Sulney	Granby-cum-Sutton	Owthorpe	Tollerton
Bulcote	Greasley	Oxton	Toton
Bulwell	Gunthorpe	Papplewick	Trowell
Bunny	Haywood Oaks	Plumtree	West Bridgford
Burton Joyce	Hickling	Radcliffe-on-Trent	West Leake
Calverton	Holme Pierrepont	Radford	Widmerpool
Carlton	Hucknall Torkard	Ratcliffe-on-Soar	Wilford
Caythorpe	Hucknall-under-Huthwaite	Rempstone	Willoughby
Chilwell	Keyworth	Ruddington	Wiverton
Clifton	Kingston-upon-Soar	Saxondale	Wollaton
Clipstone	Kinoulton	Selston	Woodborough
Colston Basset	Kirkby-in-Ashfield	Shelford	Wysall
Colwick	Lambley	Skegby	
Cossall	Lamcote	Sneinton	

2. Coroners' records

Unfortunately the records of the inquisitions of Coroner Swann have not survived; the details of those held by him from May 1828 until shortly before his death in December 1866 have been taken from the columns of the local press. These are the Nottingham Review, the Nottingham Journal and the Nottingham Mercury up to its closure in 1852. From these sources, it has been determined that during his tenure of office, Swann held 4465 inquests. It is not known how many of the inquests actually held were in fact reported in the pages of newspapers but information from the published records of Swann[7] show that he held 132 inquests from Easter to Christmas 1839 and 103 from Christmas 1839 to Michaelmas 1840. The figures abstracted from the press, are 132 and 94 respectively over the same periods and bearing in mind that the date of publication would have been some days after the event they are tolerably of the same order. Nevertheless it should not be assumed that these data are representative of the later years of press coverage, for a surviving number of accounts submitted for payment by Christopher Swann in the 1860's give a detailed list of inquests taken by him. Four out of five of these inquests were featured in newspapers at this time.

However, Swann maintained that he always fully co-operated with the press:

'*I have never kept any inquest back from the newspapers, except in cases of murder and manslaughter; nor did I ever interfere with the reporters. I have at all times, and without the slightest partiality, allowed them to have free access to the depositions in my office, and there they copy, or extract whatever they think proper, without the slightest interference on my part.*'[7]

Fortunately, a few original coroners' records from the Newark District and a larger number from the Nottingham Borough have survived and provide us with a unique source of information. These have been drawn upon to illustrate various salient points within this text.

3. Qualifications of a coroner

Writing in the Nottingham Mercury in 1836 a local medical practitioner, William Valentine, vehemently attacked the office of the coroner because persons who invariably held this position had legal but no medical training:

'*Attorneys have only been the candidates for the office of coroner. Seared by the talons of these grasping legal vultures, the unassuming votaries of medical science have shrunk from the encounter and have yielded up the field which they alone have been qualified to occupy….*'[8]

It is not surprising that this outburst greatly offended the local incumbents and it was left to Michael Browne, the coroner for the Borough of Nottingham to reply, at great length, to Valentine's '*scurrilous epithets.*'[9] At this time there was no definition of the office of coroner, the only requirement was to own land within the county. The first coroner to have a medical qualification was elected in Middlesex in 1839 but this was greeted with derision by the justices in that county. It was not until the Act of

1926 (16 & 17 Geo. V c.59) that the qualifications for coroners were formally laid down:

'*...no person shall be appointed to be a coroner... unless he is a barrister, solicitor, or legally-qualified medical practitioner, of not less than five years standing.*'

Today the majority of coroners are lawyers; others are medical men with legal training so that Valentine's assertions have never been realised in toto.

4. Financial costs of holding an inquest

Before 1487 coroners did not receive any payment for their services, for it was always regarded that the honour of holding this office was recompense enough. However by an Act of Parliament in this year (3 Hen. VII c.1) a coroner was entitled to receive 13s. 4d. '*on every inquisition taken upon the view of the body slain and murdered*'. This remuneration to be taken from '*the goods and chattels of him that is the slayer and murderer*'. A coroner received no payment for inquests (1 Hen. VIII c.7) where the person had been '*slain, drowned or otherwise dead by misadventure*'. This form of remuneration remained in place until 1752 when by a further Act (25 Geo. II c.29), an attempt was made to rationalise the system. In this legislation it was stipulated that they were to be paid 20s. for every inquisition taken in any township contributing to the county rates. The Act specifically stated that this sum was over and above the 13s. 4d. already granted, but the conditions applied to this latter sum made it virtually meaningless. In addition they were to receive 9d. for every mile they were obliged to travel from their home to the place where the inquest was held. In county districts this may have been substantial but strangely enough the cost of the return journey appears to have been ignored!

Whilst the original records of the inquests taken by Christopher Swann have not survived, his claims for fees, expenses and disbursements are available. These can be found in the minutes of the Nottinghamshire Quarter Sessions held at the Shire Hall, Nottingham over the period 1828 - 1866 and some have also survived in the County Treasurer's accounts. In addition, a number of accounts submitted by Swann in the 1860's for approval at the Quarter Sessions have been located amongst miscellaneous vouchers in the Nottinghamshire Archives. Data from these three sources have been abstracted and presented as yearly data in Table 3. During the period 1828 to 1837 Swann was paid according to the Statute of 1752 and he received 20s. for each inquest and his travelling expenses of 9d. per mile. The cost of each inquest was in the order of £1.11s. although this amount would have been slightly larger, for during this period the parish in which the inquest took place would have been expected to contribute towards any local costs incurred. At this time, medical witnesses were expected to attend inquests gratuitously but as the minutes of the Quarter Sessions and County Treasurer's accounts show, they were paid expenses. These expenses for each inquest attended, were individually claimed by every medically-qualified witness, sometimes naming the parish to which they had travelled.

The year 1836 can be recognised as marking a significant change, for an important piece of legislation was enacted (6 & 7 Will. IV c.89). It provided for the payment (£1 1s.) to medical witnesses attending coroners' inquests and for carrying out post-mortem examinations with or without analysis of the contents of the stomach and intestines (£2 2s.). For the first time coroners were also given power under this Act to order any medical practitioner to carry out such examination or to appear as a witness at an inquest, this power being exercisable by the majority of the jury.

Table 3.

The financial costs of inquests held each year by Christopher Swann from May 1828 to December 1866

Year	Swann's fee or salary	Expenses and disbursements	Total cost to the County Rate
1828	£92 5s.0d.	£4 10s.0d.	£96 15s.0d.
1829	£96 0s.9d.	£11 18s.6d.	£107 19s.3d.
1830	£103 15s.9d.	£12 9s.0d.	£116 4s.9d.
1831	£117 8s.6d.	£18 15s.0d.	£136 3s.6d.
1832	£121 2s.0d.	£27 5s.6d.	£148 7s.6d.
1833	£128 15s.6d.	£15 2s.0d.	£143 17s.6d.
1834	£132 16s.6d.	£24 0s.0d.	£156 16s.6d.
1835	£154 16s.3d.	£14 19s.0d.	£169 15s.3d.
1836	£133 13s.9d.	£25 19s.0d.	£159 12s.9d.
1837	£144 1s.2d.	£102 14s.6d.	£246 15s.8d.
1838	£208 17s.10d.	£406 12s.6d.	£615 10s.4d.
1839	£264 2s.4d.	£481 4s.8d.	£745 7s.0d.
1840	£201 4s.3d.	£321 6s.9d.	£522 11s.0d.
1841	£183 10s.8d.	£287 4s.5d.	£470 15s.1d.
1842	£226 7s.0d.	£348 0s.4d.	£574 7s.4d.
1843	£210 5s.8d.	£309 5s.10d.	£519 11s.6d.
1844	£231 9s.8d.	£366 13s.4d.	£598 3s.0d.
1845	£223 16s.7d.	£315 9s.9d.	£539 6s.4d.
1846	£219 14s.6d.	£325 6s.0d.	£545 0s.6d.
1847	£231 14s.10d.	£323 14s.4d.	£555 9s.2d.
1848	£264 12s.9d.	£237 9s.8d.	£502 2s.5d.
1849	no record	no record	£571 16s.0d.
1850	no record	no record	£620 5s.10d.
1851	no record	no record	£644 15s.0d.
1852	no record	no record	£637 2s.2d.
1853	no record	no record	£626 4s.10d.
1854	no record	no record	£483 18s.9d.
1855	no record	no record	£397 13s.6d.
1856	no record	no record	£419 8s.4d.
1857	no record	no record	£457 3s.7d.
1858	no record	no record	£354 6s.5d.
1859	no record	no record	£370 16s.6d.
1860	no record	no record	£394 9s.2d.
1861[a]	£250 0s.0d.	£183 14s.10d.	£433 14s.10d.
1862[a]	£250 0s.0d.	£152 8s.2d.	£402 8s.2d.
1863	£250 0s.0d.	£160 1s.0d.	£410 1s.0d.
1864	£250.0s.0d.	£144 12s.6d.	£394 12s.6d.
1865	£250 0s.0d.	£138 7s.6d.	£388 7s.6d.
1866	£250 0s.0d.	£111 5s.6d.	£361 5s.6d.

The financial data were taken from the minutes of the Nottinghamshire Quarter Sessions [Nottinghamshire Archives QSM 1/41-49].
Between 1849 and 1860 the fees and expenses were generally not recorded as separate figures in the minutes.
[a] From the surviving accounts of Swann [Nottinghamshire Archives QF/CT/8].

The Justices were also required to draw-up a list of expenses etc., payable on taking inquests. At a meeting of the Nottinghamshire Magistrates held at Southwell on the 26th October 1837 the schedule of fees, allowances and disbursements to be paid to and on behalf of coroners holding inquests in Nottinghamshire was issued[10] (Table 4).

Table 4.

A schedule of fees, allowances and disbursements to be paid to and on behalf of coroners holding inquests in Nottinghamshire from October 1837

Parties	Services or Duties	Allowance
Constable	Of the parish where inquest held, journey to give notice to the coroner of the death of persons – per mile	1s. for the first mile and 6d. for every extra mile
	Serving the coroner's summons on three constables of adjoining parishes and summoning two jurors in his own parish – per mile	1s. each summons serving and the same allowance as above for every mile travelling to serve them where they cannot be served on his way back from the coroner
	Attending the inquest in his own parish	1s.
Constables	Of the three adjoining parishes summoning three jurors in each parish	Any sum not exceeding 3d. each constable
Jurors	For refreshment on attending the inquest	Any sum not exceeding 2d. each juror
Witnesses	Attending to give evidence (not medical men)	Not exceeding 1s.6d. each witness necessary
Coroner	For one summons to the constable of each parish to summon jury	4s.
	Fee demanded on each inquest by the Clerk of Assize	2s.6d.
	Holding the inquest the usual fee under the old Act of Parliament	20s.
	Additional fee for other services under this and the Registration of Deaths Act	6s.8d.
	His mileage as before	9d. for each mile to the inquest

The effect of this legislation was immediate and in subsequent years there was a very marked increase in the costs of an inquest to be borne by the county rate (Table 3). It is not surprising therefore that the justices at the Quarter Sessions made every effort to reduce this expenditure. The costs of an inquest were highly dependent on:

- The distance from the coroner's office to the parish where the inquest was held, as this determined the level of his mileage claim.
- And whether or not the coroner sought the advice of a medical witness.

Shortly after its publication the interpretation of the Act sometimes led to differences of opinion.[11] On one occasion a coroner in another county refused to accede to a medical man's claim for expenses because he was only prepared to accept that a surgeon had earned a fee when a post-mortem examination had been undertaken. At another time the magistrates refused to pay expenses greater than two guineas for the analysis of stomach contents. A surviving letter from Swann to William Newton (coroner for the Newark District) cites an earlier report in Gloucestershire, when due to a technicality, a higher court upheld a similar claim. The reason being that an analysis of stomach or intestinal contents by an independent scientific person, who would not have carried out the post-mortem, came outside the meaning of the above Act. These experts would often claim ten or twenty guineas for their services.[12]

As previously mentioned, fees and expenses paid to coroners often came under close scrutiny by the magistrate's finance committee, ever anxious to limit expenditure out of the county rate, and those claims submitted by Christopher Swann were undoubtedly examined. In 1839 and again in 1840 he was accused of holding too many inquests that resulted in verdicts which came to the conclusion that the person had died a '*natural death.*'[13] These were in the region of 40% of the total number of inquests held (Table 5).

Table 5.

The number of natural deaths recorded in inquests held by Christopher Swann during the period from Easter 1839 to Michaelmas 1840

Year	Month	Number of inquests	Number of natural deaths
1839	April	16	9
	May	12	5
	June	15	8
	July	13	4
	August	13	7
	September	13	4
	October	19	10
	November	14	6
	December	17	10
1840	January	12	4
	February	11	3
	March	11	1
	April	10	2
	May	9	3
	June	10	2
	July	10	4
	August	14	5
	September	7	2
Totals		226 (235)[a]	89 (85)[a]
Natural deaths (% of the total)			39% (36%)[a]

[a] The figures in parentheses are Christopher Swann's data from the same period [Nottingham Mercury (6th November 1840), p.357.d-e.].

Swann vigorously defended his judgements when he said:

'*Believing that the magistrates, generally, are desirous of economising the resources of the county, it has ever been my desire, as far as conscientious discharge of my duty, to act in accordance with their financial views. I must be allowed to say, that I should merit their contempt was I for one moment to forget the respect due to the important judicial office which I hold, and yield up the command of my judgement into the hands of individuals who merely look at the affair as a matter of pounds, shillings and pence. There are many cases of alleged natural death that demand rigorous investigation, which if neglected would be opening a wide door for the commission of murder.*'[7]

The argument that there were too many natural death verdicts continued to roll but Swann consistently maintained that he never held an unnecessary inquest:

'*I can appeal to the constables of Lenton, Radford, Sneinton, Carlton and various other parishes to prove that I have frequently declined holding an inquest because I considered it unnecessary.*'[13]

However, criticism sometimes came from members of the public, for as James Wells wrote concerning an inquest that was held on the body of his son, Thomas aged 14 months, at Radford on the 20th November 1839 where a verdict of '*natural death*' was recorded:

'*This little afflicted babe was the tenth child of my wife and myself. Six of them are still living and I should have expected that the natural tenderness of my wife as a parent ought to have shielded her from the torture which has been occasioned by this shameful and unnecessary waste of public money. My little son was prematurely hurried into life and was exceedingly delicate and my wonder was not at his death but that he has been kept alive for 14 months and might have lived had he escaped the measles. .... The following Tuesday the child died and in the afternoon of the same day the chief constable of Radford came to my house and made such inquiries, as he thought necessary. He was fully answered as stated above, which I think would have satisfied most people possessing common sense; but it appears that it did not satisfy the chief constable of Radford and an inquest was accordingly held. That it was vexatiously unnecessary I think no one will attempt to deny. The motive of the individual for thus disturbing the peace of a family and giving trouble to twelve persons on that occasion, I am at a loss to imagine.*'[14]

Furthermore, comments on the verdict '*Natural Causes*' came from another quarter. Henry C. Attenburrow, Honorary Secretary to the British Medical Association writing from his address in Castle Gate, Nottingham in April 1839, was highly censorious of some of these verdicts. His contention was that Swann had not called in medical expertise and he cited a number of recent decisions.

In the first: '*the child was quite well at nine p.m. taking the breast two or three times in the night and was found dead in the morning. No cause of death was assigned.*'

In the second: '*the child died after having a piece of turnip forced down its throat but from the symptoms very likely into the windpipe, by an unqualified and illegal practitioner, who subsequently attended it. Surely this was a proper case for medical investigation, were it only for the purpose of protecting the public against the mischievous interference of ignorant and irregular practitioners.*'

In the third: '*a child died in convulsions from some cause not ascertained.*'

In the fourth: '*a boy aged fourteen was admitted as medical witness and undertakes to swear that his father had not, in any way poisoned himself.*'

In conclusion Attenburrow stated that: '*if the inquest is necessary, let the inquiry be at least as perfect as possible; for what can be the use of a tribunal, where a false economy deprives the public of the safety attending a complete investigation.*'[15]

However, the criticisms of Attenburrow should not be seen as an attack on Coroner Swann but on the lamentable system that prevailed at the time. The Act of 1836 (6 & 7 Will. IV c.89) that allowed medical witnesses to be paid gave him powers to order any medical practitioner to carry out an autopsy and toxicological examination and then to appear as a witness at the inquest. Penalties could be applied to doctors who failed to comply with that order. This would seem to be an ideal solution for improving the status of an inquest but there were a number of problems that were to impede progress. The payment of medical witnesses was to be made out of funds raised for the relief of the poor. This was soon found to be an unsatisfactory arrangement and it required a further Act in 1837 (7 Will. IV & 1 Vict. c.68) to provide for the expenses of medical witnesses to be taken out of the county rate. However, the justices at the Quarter Sessions retained the power to examine coroners on oath regarding their accounts. Although the aforementioned Act provided for an additional sum of 6s. 8d. to be paid for each inquisition taken, it also decreed that the coroner must settle the expenses of witnesses, medical and otherwise, at the end of the hearing.

This did not always, at least in the initial years, have the desired effect of facilitating the attendance of medical witnesses at inquests. Faced with the reality that the coroner was obliged to pay witnesses out of his own pocket and having no assurance that the justices would approve his accounts he was perhaps reluctant to request medical expertise except in situations of obvious violence.

Whilst Attenburrow's criticisms were sound, in reality Christopher Swann must have been very frustrated by the attitude of the justices who in actuality controlled his income. Nevertheless as we have seen he was vociferous in his condemnation of a system which facilitated the promotion of secret homicide particularly in children. It was not until 1860, with the publication of the County Coroner's Act (23 & 24 Vict. c.116), which placed coroners on a salaried basis, that they gained some measure of independence from the justices.

From the 1st January 1861 County, but not Borough Coroners, received an annual salary in lieu of the fees, mileage and allowances which they previously claimed (23 & 24 Vict. c.116). This was fixed at a level of the reward they would have received in fees etc., taken as an average, over the previous five years and paid quarterly out of the county rate. It was to be reviewed every five years and would be dependent on the number of inquests held by each coroner. In 1861 Swann's remuneration was £250:

'*The average, for the Nottingham District, appeared to your committee to be £236 12s. 4d. but the coroner for that district makes it £241, which they think may be correct. Looking at the yearly increasing population of this district, your committee thinks it would be reasonable to fix the salary at £250.*'[16]

The salary of the coroner of the Retford District was fixed at £83 and that for Newark £43 reflecting the smaller population and lower number of inquests held in these areas. The coroner of the Newark District also received an additional quarterly payment as compensation for the reduction in the size of his territory in the 1858 reorganisation (page 4).

As previously mentioned the detailed claims submitted by Christopher Swann to the Justices for the recovery of his expenses, which had already been paid by him at the conclusion of an inquest, have survived for the years 1861-62. They give the place of each inquest and the name of the deceased person, and the fees paid to:

- The jury (each juror received 1s.)
- The ordinary witnesses (the usual fee was 1s. 6d.)
- The medical witnesses (they were paid £1 1s.)
- The surgeon for carrying out a post-mortem examination (the fee was £2 2s.)
- The fee demanded by an analytical chemist for an examination of body fluids
- Incidental expenses for example, hire of a room for an inquest (other than those in public houses which were provided gratis), burial of an unknown person and provision of a coffin, transporting a body to the place of the inquest etc.

Thirteen jurors were routinely required to attend an inquest but occasionally this may have been increased to 14 or 15, these numbers over the statutory 12 allowed for non-attendance in case of illness. The accounts show that in 1861 Swann held 114 inquests and 107 in 1862. During these two years, 180 of these 221 inquests (81%) were reported in the newspapers.

The salary of Swann was now fixed at £250 per annum and replaced his mileage and other payments of earlier years and provided that expense claims were receipted by each recipient there appeared to be little interference from the justices in reimbursing him. A summary of these is given in Table 6.

Table 6.

The costs of carrying out inquests by Christopher Swann in 1861 and 1862: which include his claims for expenses and his annual salary

	1861	**1862**
Number of inquests	114 (98)[a]	107 (82)[a]
Payments to the jurors	£85 18s. 0d.	£76 3s. 0d.
Ordinary witnesses expenses	£5 8s. 10d.	£8 0s. 2d.
Medical witnesses expenses	£33 12s. 0d.	£37 16s. 0d.
Cost of post-mortem examinations	£27 6s. 0d.	£30 9s. 0d.
Cost of analytical evaluations	£31 10s. 0d.	none
Swann's salary	£250 0s. 0d.	£250 0s. 0d.
Total cost of inquests	£433 14s 10d.	£402 8s. 2d.
Mean cost of each inquest	£3 16s.	£3 15s.

[a] The figures in parentheses are the number of inquests reported in the local newspapers.

The costs of requesting analysis of body fluids and examination of viscera were usually quite high and Swann only used this service on two occasions during 1861-2:

- An inquest was held in Tythby in May 1861 on the body of Nathaniel Miles. Rumours circulated in the village that he had been poisoned. This appeared to have prompted the attending surgeons to submit parts of his intestine for analysis, presumably with the coroner's permission. They were sent to Dr. Taylor in London, who charged £21 for this work, the results of which dispelled any idea that poison was implicated in the death of Miles.

- The second occasion on which samples were sent for analysis was during the inquest held at Strelley in July/August 1861, on the body of Elizabeth Bradley, who had accidentally died in an attempt to procure an abortion by taking corrosive sublimate. The charge for this service was £10 10s.

Although we are not privileged with sight of the verdicts in the above accounts of Swann they do give us a precise number of inquests he held in these two years. From the financial data we may determine the mean cost of an inquest in 1861 and 1862 (Table 6.) these are similar to those contained in the report of the Registrar General (page 90). These costs were of course highly influenced by the number of occasions on which medical personnel were called to give evidence or to carry out a post-mortem and very much inflated by requesting an expert analytical procedure.

II. THE CORONER'S COURT

It was usually the parish constable who would inform Coroner Swann that a person had died in a parish under his jurisdiction and that he thought the death was possibly not due to natural causes. However, from the 2nd January 1854 the parish constables were relieved of these duties which passed to the County Police:

'That in future the County Police be directed to take upon themselves the duties of summoning the coroner and jury in all inquests and that the coroners be informed that in future the allowances to Parish Constables for such duties be discontinued.'[17]

Either the parish constable or the County Police had to travel to Swann's office in Castle Gate, Nottingham to make their report. Swann would carefully study the evidence presented to him and then would decide whether or not an inquiry was in order. He would need to accept that there was reasonable cause to suspect that the person had died either:

(a) A violent or an unnatural death, or
(b) A sudden death, of which the cause was unknown, or
(c) In such a place or under such circumstances as to require an inquest (for instance in prison, in a hospital, workhouse or lunatic asylum).

The reason for holding inquests on persons dying in public institutions was to satisfy relatives and acquaintances that they had received proper medical care and attention.

Holding an inquest required some degree of organisation that would fall to the Coroner's Officer in co-operation with the relevant parish officer or the County Police. A number of other persons would be summoned to attend, including the jury, ordinary witnesses, possibly medical witnesses and/or medically-qualified persons to carry out a post-mortem examination of the body of the deceased and perhaps perform an analysis of the stomach or intestinal contents. Others indirectly involved would be those providing or organising the provision of accommodation, for instance a publican or the parish clerk.

1. The jury

If an inquest were to be held then the coroner would issue a warrant to inquire into the death and to summon a jury at a time and place of his choosing. The warrant given to the parish constable or the County Police would probably be similar to that issued in 1801 by George Hodgkinson, one of the coroners for Nottinghamshire, to the Constable of Halam.[18] The rules for the selection of jurors under the Statute of 1825 (6 Geo. IV c.22), because they needed to be called together in haste, could not apply to coroners' juries. Nevertheless, attempts were made to

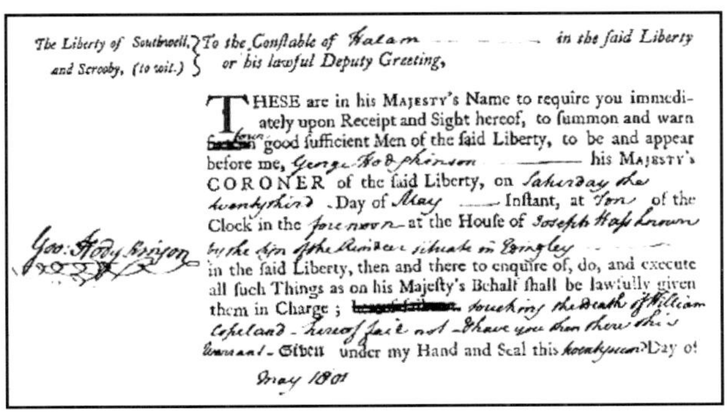
The Liberty of Southwell, and Scrooby, (to wit.) To the Constable of Halam in the said Liberty or his lawful Deputy Greeting,

THESE are in his MAJESTY's Name to require you immediately upon Receipt and Sight hereof, to summon and warn [illegible] good sufficient Men of the said Liberty, to be and appear before me, George Hodgkinson his MAJESTY's CORONER of the said Liberty, on Saturday the twentythird Day of May Instant, at Ten of the Clock in the forenoon at the House of Joseph [illegible] known by the sign of the [illegible] situate in [illegible] in the said Liberty, then and there to enquire of, do, and execute all such Things as on his Majesty's Behalf shall be lawfully given them in Charge; touching the death of William Copeland - hereof fail not - & have you then there this Warrant - Given under my Hand and Seal this twentysecond Day of May 1801

Geo: Hodgkinson

An example of a warrant issued by a coroner to a parish constable requiring him to select a jury for an inquest summon '*good and lawful men*' between the ages of twenty-one and sixty. The jury would usually be composed of men from the constable's own and two adjoining parishes and consist of a minimum of twelve persons. A greater number would initially be chosen to allow for any that may for good reason, usually illness, not be able to serve. A jury was made-up of freeholders, provided that:

'*…no man who has been or shall be attained of any treason or felony or convicted of any crime that is infamous, unless he shall have obtained a free pardon.*'

Jurors were usually expected to be literate men but particularly in rural areas this may have been difficult to accomplish as noted at an inquest which took place at Screveton as late as 1898 where two jurors were unable to sign the inquisition.[19] An inquest had to be held at the place where '*the body lay dead*'; although it may well have been that the death had occurred elsewhere, for example a person may have drowned many miles from where the body was discovered in a river.

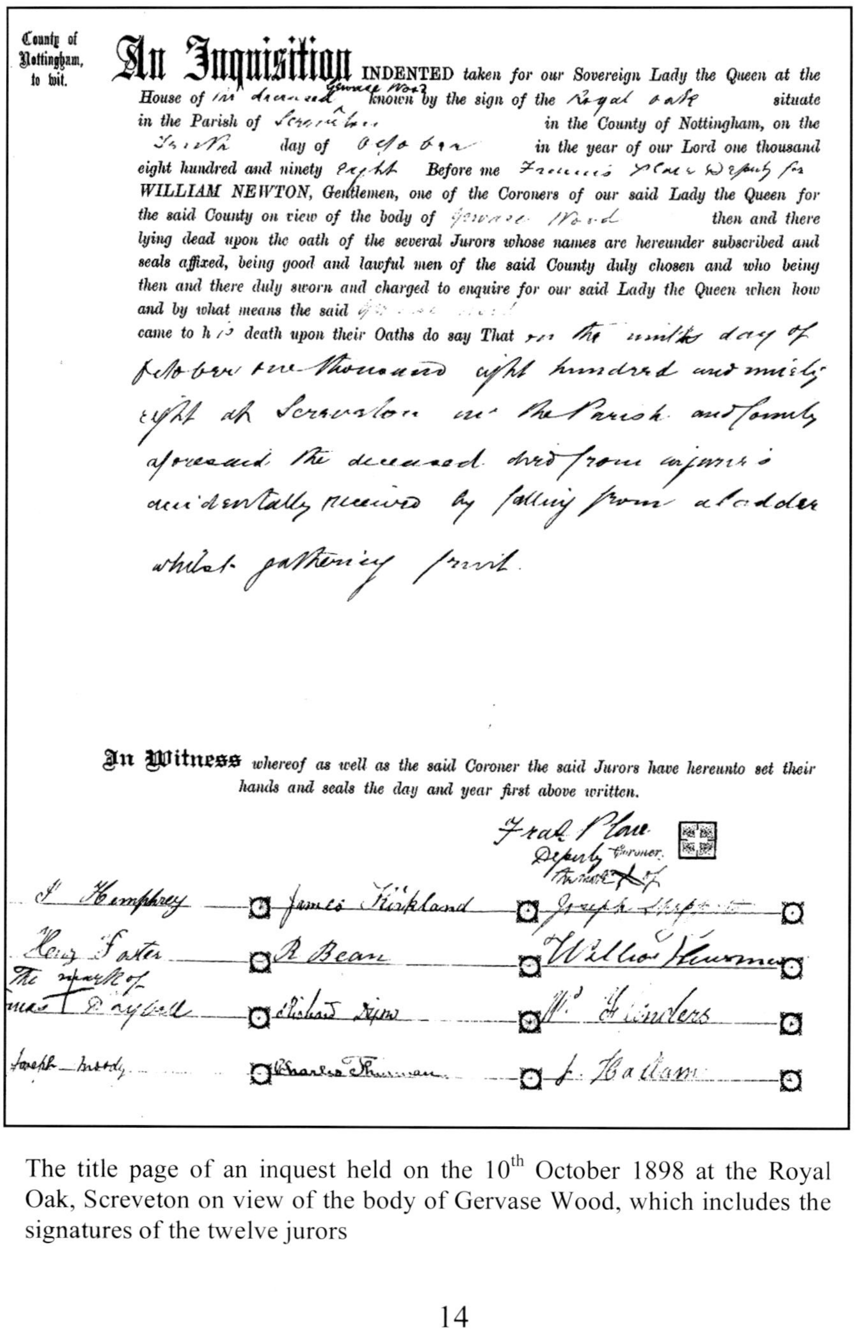
County of Nottingham, to wit.

An Inquisition INDENTED *taken for our Sovereign Lady the Queen at the House of* the deceased Gervase Wood *known by the sign of the* Royal Oak *situate in the Parish of* Screveton *in the County of Nottingham, on the* Tenth *day of* October *in the year of our Lord one thousand eight hundred and ninety* eight *Before me* Francis Place Deputy for *WILLIAM NEWTON, Gentlemen, one of the Coroners of our said Lady the Queen for the said County on view of the body of* Gervase Wood *then and there lying dead upon the oath of the several Jurors whose names are hereunder subscribed and seals affixed, being good and lawful men of the said County duly chosen and who being then and there duly sworn and charged to enquire for our said Lady the Queen when how and by what means the said* Gervase Wood *came to* his *death upon their Oaths do say That* on the ninth day of October one thousand eight hundred and ninety eight at Screveton in the Parish and County aforesaid the deceased died from injuries accidentally received by falling from a ladder whilst gathering fruit.

In Witness *whereof as well as the said Coroner the said Jurors have hereunto set their hands and seals the day and year first above written.*

Frank Place
Deputy Coroner

J. Humphrey — James Kirkland — Joseph [illegible]
Henry Foster — R Bean — William [illegible]
The mark of [illegible] — [illegible] — W. Saunders
Joseph [illegible] — Charles Thurman — J. Hallam

The title page of an inquest held on the 10th October 1898 at the Royal Oak, Screveton on view of the body of Gervase Wood, which includes the signatures of the twelve jurors

2. Viewing the body

After the jury had been sworn they had to view the body that would invariably have been taken into a public house; the coroner would also take the opportunity to make any points that he wished the jury to consider. At one time it was usual for the deceased to be on view during the whole of the proceedings but during Swann's tenure this was no longer necessary and the corpse would lie in an adjoining room or in an out-house. In order that the jury were not too offended by the procedure, attempts were made to make the body as presentable as possible for their inspection. However, in cases of violent or the more extreme accidental deaths from mechanical injury this must have been difficult:

'*On Saturday the 15th January 1858 an inquest was held at the Cranmer Arms, Aslockton, touching the death of Thomas Lane, aged 70, rag gatherer of Scarrington. It appears from the evidence that on Friday morning the deceased was proceeding along the footpath from Aslockton to Whatton and when crossing the line about 120 yards from Aslockton station he was knocked down by the engine of a train... The train was stopped as soon as possible and the guard, William Stones, going back along the track found the body of the deceased in a very mangled state. Both his legs were off, and a portion of his body and clothes were lying on different parts of the ground for eighteen yards, the distance the body had been driven by the train.* ***The body was collected together and brought to the public house where the inquest was held****....*'[20]

Cranmer Arms, Aslockton (1973)

Likewise, the jury at an inquest held some years earlier, on Friday 10th November 1832 at the Three Crowns, Bulwell was similarly faced with viewing a corpse in a dreadful state. A young boy aged between 13 and 14 years had gone into a bleach mill to look for his sister who worked there and accidentally fell into the machinery. The mill was stopped as soon as possible but by then he had become entangled between two sets of spur-wheels that were revolving between each other:

Three Crowns, Bulwell (1998)

'*...the body was cut entirely in two, one half being brought out first, then the other half and afterwards the bowels, parts of bones and different portions of his clothing...* ***The various parts of the body had been collected together for the inspection of the jury*** *and presented a most shocking spectacle.*'[21]

Publicans were not always willing to provide the most appropriate room for the reception of the body of an unfortunate person who had met an unexplained death. William Sears appears to have had little respect for the body of John Kirkwood who met a brutal death in Carrington on Monday 15th August 1842:

'*The body lay in "the coal-house" of the William Fourth Inn and on the jury taking a view of it, presented an appearance of foul play. A heavy wound being on the left temple, as if produced by a brick or large stone having been thrown at the head of Kirkwood....*'[22]

It was imperative that all the members of the jury were able to view the body of the deceased. Sometimes a problem arose if for instance, during an adjournment of an inquest one of the jurymen died, it was then necessary for his replacement to also see the body. If a funeral had already taken place then unfortunately for the relatives, the deceased person would be disinterred.

On the 20th August 1858 the boiler of a steam-threshing machine at Daybrook exploded; seven men were injured but one man, Joseph Stevenson lost his life. The catastrophe was attributable to the neglect of Henry Sulley, the fireman, failing to ease the safety valve. But as he was so severely injured he had to be taken to the General Hospital in Nottingham; the inquest which opened soon after the incident, was adjourned until Sulley was able to attend. The inquiry was not concluded until the 2nd December when Sulley had so far recovered as to be able, by walking on crutches, to attend the adjourned inquest at the Black Swan in Daybrook. The additional evidence was first taken:

Black Swan, Daybrook (c.1890)

'Luke Teather said I live at Sherwood and I am the sexton at Carrington church. I was present when Joseph Stevenson was buried on the 22nd August 1858. On the 19th November I opened the grave again and showed the coffin containing the corpse to the jurymen (one of the original jurors having died since the inquest was adjourned). As a fresh one was appointed in his place, it became necessary as a legal form to exhume the body, so that the new juror might have the "view" of it. George Terry, wheelwright of Daybrook, said I made the coffin and assisted to place the body in it. At the funeral the last witness helped me lower the coffin into the grave. I am sure the body found is that of the deceased who was killed at Daybrook.'[23]

3. Identifying the body

An inquest could not take place without a body, which after being viewed by the jury, would be formally identified. Although sometimes doubts of identification might arise, as recounted by Swann at an inquest in 1863:

'Some years ago I had occasion to hold an inquest in Sneinton on the body of a girl who had been found drowned. A servant girl was missing at the time and the father of this girl and some of her companions examined the body, and were quite confident that it was that of the missing girl. They identified it by certain marks on the hands. The girl's master could not be convinced and he stoutly maintained that she would never drown herself. The inquiry was twice adjourned in order to get further evidence of identification and the girls' relations were still confident and her master incredulous. At the third sitting the coroner was busy taking down the evidence when the door was opened and the missing girl walked into the room and coolly addressing the coroner said, "I understand, Sir, that you are holding an inquest on me." The astonishment of all assembled may be imagined and the girl's master was so much affected that he sank from his chair crying but he just managed to articulate "You see I was right Sir." The relatives were of course glad to be convinced so forcibly of their mistake and the coroner had to seek other identifiers on the body actually found.'[24, 25]

4. The venue

The venue for the inquest was invariably either a public house or after the passing of the Beer Act of 1830 (11 Geo. IV & 1 Will. IV c.64) occasionally one of the retail beer houses which were opening in the county. These two types of licensed premises accounted for at least 95% of the chosen venues. Other premises sometimes used were schoolrooms, parish churches, the General Hospital, the County Gaol, workhouses, the Lunatic Asylum or private residences. Whilst it was incumbent on the selected jurors to attend on the nominated day at the appointed time, publicans were not obliged to give over part of their premises for an inquest although most were happy to do so. They would ordinarily not receive any remuneration for letting-out their rooms but they were all too well aware that additional revenue, in the form of post-inquest eating and drinking, would invariably be forthcoming. This long-established perquisite sometimes prompted caustic letters to be addressed to the local press:

'*The scene of intoxication which has been exhibited at a coroner's inquest in this county, latterly (after the coroner had departed), has induced me to offer a few brief remarks. That the drunkenness which is not infrequently observed after a solemn enquiry regarding the unhappy death of a fellow creature upon a coroner's inquest is an absolute disgrace to the country which we live in. I think but few, if any (save the sots themselves), will be found to deny....*'[26]

Others proposed that a coroner's inquest should not take place on licensed premises and offered alternative suggestions to funding this very important judicial inquiry. However, the writer had to wait over 70 years until an Act of Parliament (2 Edw. VII c.28 s.21) published in 1902 curtailed the use of such venues:

'*From and after the thirty-first day of March one thousand nine hundred and seven no meeting of justices in petty or special sessions shall be held in premises licensed for the sale of intoxicating liquors. ... Nor shall any coroner's inquest be held on such licensed premises, where other suitable premises have been provided for such inquest.*'

On the 8th of January 1906 Coroner D. Whittingham held an inquest at the Trent Bridge Inn, West Bridgford on the body of a man who had been killed in an accident involving a motor car which had apparently startled the horse of the deceased.[27] At the end of the inquest the coroner remarked that there should be a proper place for holding inquests in West Bridgford. Nevertheless it is believed that a public house was occasionally used as a venue for holding inquests for some time to come.

Occasionally publicans refused to take a dead body into their public house but in so doing they ran the risk of incurring the wrath of the local constabulary and magistrates for in 1856:

'*The licence of William Carver, publican of Wilford was suspended for a period of twelve months by the magistrates for refusing, on the application of a police officer, to allow the dead body of a young gentleman who was drowned in the Trent this summer to be in his house.*'[28]

Carver did however, consent to the holding of the inquest in his public house, the Punch Bowl at Wilford, but in the meanwhile the body of John Clarke had been taken to the belfry of the parish church where presumably it was on view for the jury.[29]

An inquest must take place at a venue that was situated within the district over which the coroner had jurisdiction, furthermore the deceased must have died, or the body discovered, within that district. The boundaries between two districts may on occasions cause problems. This is amply illustrated by the boundary between the parish of West Bridgford and that of St Mary's, Nottingham. The former was in the district controlled by Coroner Swann whilst the latter was under the jurisdiction of the Coroner for the borough:

'*An inquest was held on the 20th November 1829 at the Three Horse Shoes public house, which was sited near Trent Bridge on the body of Albert Polak. He died after being thrown from his horse on the road approaching Nottingham from the South and his body was taken into the Three Horse Shoes* (permanently renamed the Trent Bridge Inn by 1842). *An inquest was held before Jonathan Dunn, one of the coroners for the Borough of Nottingham. However, in the meantime the Parish Constable for West Bridgford had informed Christopher Swann that there had been a fatal accident in this parish. On the following day another inquest was held in a different part of the Three Horse Shoes before Coroner Swann which reached a similar verdict. Apparently the boundary between the county and the borough ran through the public house. Mrs. Chapman, landlady of the Three Horse Shoes said that she paid Parish Rates to St. Mary's, Nottingham and to West Bridgford. The door, the bar, the little parlour on the left-hand side, the north corner of the parlour and part of the kitchen were in St. Mary's Parish, the remainder was in the Parish of West Bridgford. She had no doubt the place of the accident was in the county and the body when taken into her house was not at any time within the Liberties of the town of Nottingham.*'[30]

Coroner Swann held a number of inquests in subsequent years at the Trent Bridge Inn but he was always careful to ensure that the jury was sitting in that part of the public house that was in the county:

'*Some amusement was created by several of the jurors having to leave one end of the room where they had seated themselves, because they were sitting in the Borough of Nottingham.*'[31]

5. Witnesses

The number of witnesses called to testify depended on the complexity of the proceedings and would vary from only one or two in a more straightforward case to much larger numbers in complex situations, for instance, when foul play was suspected. If it was established that death was likely to be due to murder or manslaughter, a coroner's warrant would be issued and the alleged perpetrator(s) would be committed for trial, usually at the next Assize Court.

It must have been very difficult for a coroner to write down the evidence given by some witnesses. He would have to cope with the natural language of the people and the colloquial expressions they would use. It is perhaps fortunate that a sharp legal mind was particularly suited to this aspect of his duties.

These statements from witnesses, both from a surgeon and others, who would be brought before the coroner to give their testimony of the events prior to or subsequent to the death of the deceased, would be written out on a form which was materially little changed throughout the nineteenth century.

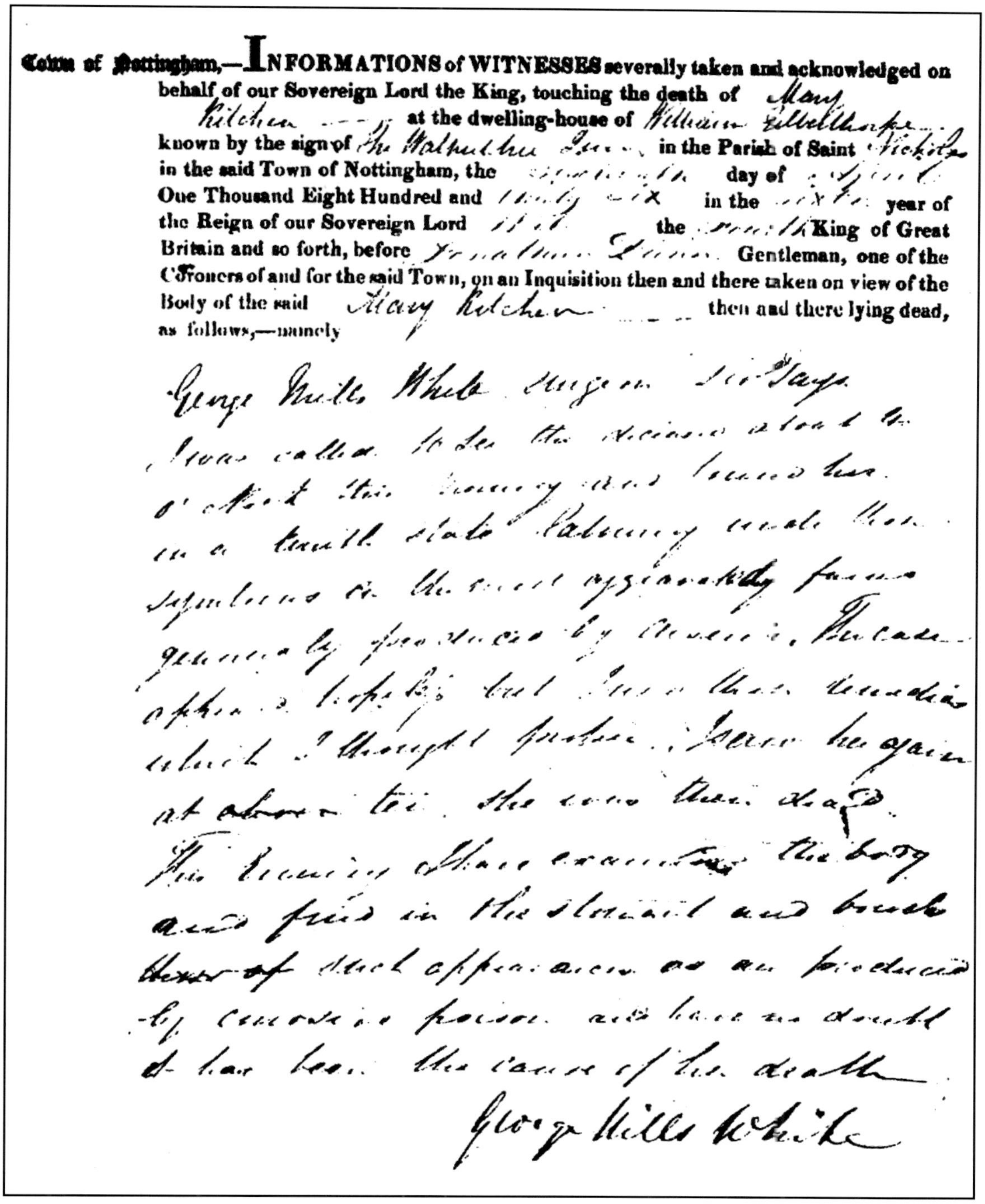

Town of Nottingham,—INFORMATIONS of WITNESSES severally taken and acknowledged on behalf of our Sovereign Lord the King, touching the death of Mary Kitchen at the dwelling-house of William [illegible] known by the sign of The Walnut tree [illegible] in the Parish of Saint Nicholas in the said Town of Nottingham, the seventeenth day of April One Thousand Eight Hundred and thirty six in the sixth year of the Reign of our Sovereign Lord William the fourth King of Great Britain and so forth, before Jonathan Dunn Gentleman, one of the Coroners of and for the said Town, on an Inquisition then and there taken on view of the Body of the said Mary Kitchen then and there lying dead, as follows,—namely

George Mills White Surgeon saith I was called to see the deceased about 4 o'clock this morning and found her in a trembling state labouring under those symptoms in the most aggravated form generally produced by arsenic, the case appeared hopeless but I used those remedies which I thought prudent. I saw her again at about ten she was then dead. This morning I have examined the body and find in the stomach and bowels thereof such appearances as are produced by corrosive poison and I have no doubt it has been the cause of her death.

George Mills White

An example of a form on which the coroner would record the statements made by witnesses at an inquest[32]

6. The verdict

The verdict of the jury and their names and signatures was recorded separately from the witness statements. An example of the coroners' records from the Newark County Division later in the century is shown on page 14.

In more serious cases the jury would be conducted to another room in order to make their deliberations but they would be expected to arrive at a unanimous verdict. Indeed it was the custom to deprive them of heat, food and light until they had come to a decision.[33]

7. Deodand

Deodand is derived from Deo dandum '*to be given to God*' and was used to designate the instrument or more usually its value, whether it was an animal or an inanimate object, which had caused the death of a person. A coroner's court often applied a deodand and the funds so generated were originally forfeited to the Sovereign or the Church, but latterly they went into the coffers of the county or borough. It was abolished on the 1st September 1846, by an Act of Parliament (9 & 10 Vict. c.62.). There are many examples where this was applied during the early years of Swann's tenure and although its value was usually small it could be huge as a result of a major incident:

Brick and Tile, Underwood (1998)

'On the 5th November 1834 an inquest was held at the Brick and Tile, Underwood, on view of the body of William Richards aged six years. On the previous Friday afternoon a man was in charge of some waggons of coal which were being drawn along a gangway by means of a whimsey at a colliery in Selston. He saw the deceased and two other children cross over the gangway and immediately afterwards he heard a scream. He then saw the deceased lying on the ground with his thigh under one of the waggon wheels. The boy had been attempting to climb on the waggon in order to ride when he slipped. The flesh was torn from below his knee to the top of his thigh. He lingered to the following Monday when he died. Verdict: Accidental death ***with a deodand of sixpence on the waggon****.'*[34]

Plough, Hickling (1997)

'On the 8th August 1845 an inquest was held at the Plough, Hickling, on view of the body of Jane Buttery aged 82 years. On the previous day John Hardy of Hickling, farmer was riding a mare around his farm tending his sheep. At one point he dismounted and tethered the horse to a hedge. Unfortunately the animal broke loose and a branch from the hedge remained attached to her halter. This seems to have caused the creature to panic and she galloped towards home. In so doing colliding with Jane Buttery who was walking along the road. The mare's hind feet struck the deceased and became entangled in her clothing dragging the unfortunate woman some way along the road. A witness, William Simpson, said that she appeared to be dead, when he found her. She had received a blow to the back of her head, which caused her death.

Verdict: Accidentally killed ***and the jury imposed a deodand of sixpence upon the mare the property of Robert Hardy of Hickling, farmer.*** '[35]

In the closing weeks of 1844 there was a collision between two trains on the Midland Railway near the station at Beeston. A large number of persons were injured, some seriously. Unfortunately two persons died from injuries they received in this accident. One person was taken to Nottingham where he died in the General Hospital and the Borough Coroner carried out an inquest. The inquest on the body of the other person, William Varnalls, was held by Christopher Swann, initially at the Three Wheat Sheaves in Lenton and by adjournment at the Shire Hall, Nottingham, where after the jury had deliberated for over eight hours they then pronounced:

'*We return a verdict of accidental death and impose a* ***deodand of £1000 upon the engine, tenders and carriages being the property of the Midland Railway.***'[36]

8. The day of the inquest – Sunday

The functions of the coroner's office are ministerial and judicial and whilst he may perform his ministerial duties, such as issuing his warrant for summoning a jury upon a Sunday, any judicial act on his part ought not to be performed. Consequently the taking of an inquisition or viewing a body would be void.[1]

Christopher Swann appears to have been unaware of this ruling or more likely he chose on some occasions to disregard it, for according to reports in the local press, a number of his inquests were held on this traditional day of rest. This may have been due to pressure of work or perhaps the ease of summoning a jury on a non-working day. However, it appears that the validity of these verdicts was never challenged:

Blue Bell, Sutton-in-Ashfield (1998)

'***On Sunday the 12th November 1837****, at the Blue Bell, Sutton-in-Ashfield, on the body of Elizabeth Didsberry, aged 34 years. The deceased and two friends had been on a jaunt of pleasure, on Wednesday last, from Mansfield to Kirkby. On their return, the same night, the driver took a corner too soon, one of the wheels hit a stone on the side of the road, and he was thrown out. The horse finding itself at liberty ran off at full gallop and the deceased was also thrown from the gig and was so severely injured as to cause her death on Friday. The horse was not stopped until it had got nearly as far as Mansfield, having at the time only part of the shafts attached to the harness. Verdict: Accidental death.*'[37].

Wheatsheaf, Cropwell Bishop (c.1960)

'***On Sunday the 17th August 1862****, at the Wheatsheaf, Cropwell Bishop, touching the death of George Simpson, aged 27 years. The deceased worked for Mr. Abbott, farmer, and about one o'clock in the afternoon of the previous Sunday he went out shooting birds on the farm. He returned about quarter-past two and said he had caught the gun against a stile and it had exploded and shot him in the arm. His left arm was much injured and medical attendance of Mr. Marriott, of Colston Basset, was promptly obtained. The deceased had lost much blood, lingered through the week, but died about seven o'clock on Saturday morning. Verdict: Died from an accidental gunshot wound.*'[38]

9. The day of the inquest – Christmas Day

No restrictions appeared to apply to holding inquests on Christmas Day, provided it did not fall on a Sunday. There were a number of occasions when Swann would summon a jury to appear on this day and it could not have been a popular decision for the twelve men and the others involved. In 1865 he held two inquests on that day:[39]

'***On Christmas Day an inquest was held by Mr. Swann**, at the Trent Bridge Inn, West Bridgford over the body of a middle-aged woman found drowned in the Trent on Saturday. The body was discovered by a man named Hind when walking by the riverside, near the osier holt, opposite the Trent Baths, the clothes of the deceased having caught one of the piles in the water. With the assistance of police constable Bingley and the bath keeper the body was got out. The bath keeper recollected having seen the woman walking on the riverside between four and five o'clock on Thursday. Her arms were bare and she appeared to be in a state of destitution. While the inquest was being held Edwin Stanley, a framework knitter, at Sneinton went to look at the body and recognised it as that of a female named Maria Burrows. She was a single woman and about fifty years of age. Twenty-seven years ago she lived in the Meadow-platts, Nottingham and ten or a dozen years since she cohabited with a man named Timms, who Stanley believed was now dead. She obtained a living by begging and prostitution. She had a brother, a framework knitter at Sutton-in-Ashfield, but Stanley did not know if he was still alive. The jury returned a verdict of: Found drowned*'.

Trent Bridge Inn, West Bridgford (c.1842)

'***On Christmas Day Mr. Swann held an inquest** at the Anchor, Gunthorpe, over the body of Kate Isabella Elliott, a child of four years old. She was the illegitimate daughter of a young woman who died at Radford some time ago. When very young the child was put out to nurse with the wife of John Blatherwick of Gunthorpe. On the 21st instant the little girl went to play with Hancock's child next door to Blatherwick's and unobserved by Mrs. Hancock went and drank boiling water from the spout of the kettle as it stood on the hob. The child's screams attracted the attention of Mrs. Blatherwick, as well as Mrs. Hancock, to whom the little sufferer said what she had done innocently adding "I won't do so any more". The usual remedies were applied but at eleven o'clock the next night [Friday] the child died. The jury returned a verdict of: Accidental death, through inhaling steam from boiling water in a kettle*'.

Anchor, Gunthorpe (1998)

III. THE INQUESTS OF CORONER SWANN 1828 – 1866

Christopher Swann was elected as a Nottinghamshire Coroner on Thursday 15th of May 1828 and by the following Tuesday 20th of May he held his first inquest at the Unicorn public house in Gunthorpe, on the body of a man who had been found in the river Trent:

'Edmund Godfrey, the Gunthorpe ferry-man, recognised the body to be that of John Grocock, boatman of Gunthorpe, whom he had ferried over the Trent in his boat after 10 o'clock on the preceding Monday evening. The deceased was rather in liquor, he said "good night" and walked away towards East Bridgford, without reeling or staggering. Samuel Turner of Newark was steering Mr. Hubbard's boat down the Trent on Sunday morning when he discovered the body near the Willow Holme. Mr. B.W. Wright, surgeon of East Bridgford, had examined the body of the deceased and found a contusion over the left eye, which he believed was occasioned by falling on a stone. It would stun the deceased so that if he fell into the water, he would be unable to help himself; there were no other marks of violence on the body. Verdict: Found drowned.'[40]

On Friday of that week Swann travelled to Sutton-in-Ashfield where he presided at an inquest on the body of Mary Houseley who being of unsound mind died as a result of cutting her throat; this was his first case of suicide. On the same day he was in the parish of Radford where an elderly woman, Mary Bailey, had accidentally died from choking and suffocation.[41]

With a large district to cover, Swann must have found that transport to the more remote parishes presented him with difficulties. In those early years, before the railway network was established, travel by some of the poorly maintained roads was the only option. We know that on occasions he opted to use the stagecoach but it was more than likely he went to an inquest from his office in Nottingham using his personal gig. In later years, wherever possible, he would take advantage of the more cost effective train services.

During this period of our history the death rate in children, more particularly in the poorer working classes, was high and many succumbed to one of the more prevalent diseases such as scarlet fever. However, only a few of these deaths were suspicious and the majority would not therefore have been subjected to a coroner's inquest. Approximately one in three deaths examined by Christopher Swann occurred in children under nine years of age. The main causes of these juvenile fatalities coming to the notice of the coroner were from severe burns, from scalding with boiling water or accidental overdose of preparations containing opium. Children also died from drowning, suffocation in bed or as a result of accidents on the roads or in the workplace etc. Deaths in the adult population (over 21 years) accounted for 59% of the total and also included verdicts of suicide, manslaughter and murder.

The 4465 inquests held by Coroner Swann during the 38 years that he was in office, which were recorded in the local press, have been classified into groups according to the reported verdicts; they are listed in Table 7. From several of these groupings a cross-section have been selected for more detailed examination.

Table 7.

Classification of the verdicts given by the jury at the close of inquests taken by Christopher Swann between May 1828 and December 1866

Group according to a coroner's verdict	Description	Number of inquests[a]
Abortion	Died as a result of attempts to terminate a pregnancy	8
Animal accident	Died when a horse, cow, bull, ram or dog was involved	61
Balloon accident	Died due to the falling of a balloon	1
Burnt or scalded	Died from accidental burns or scalds	534
Cart accident	Killed on the road, usually run over	195
Child-birth	Mother or child died at the time of child-birth	21
Choking	Accidentally died from choking, usually on food	18
Coach accident	Run over by a stage coach	3
Coal-mine accident	Died at a coal-mine, usually from a roof fall or an explosion	197
Drowned	Accidentally drowned or found drowned in a river, canal etc.	354
Exposure	Died from exposure to the weather or lack of care and attention	37
Fever	Died from an infectious disease, e.g. cholera, typhus etc.	25
Field accident	Died in a field or in the street, including struck by lightning	41
Fighting	Accidentally died in a fight	7
Found dead	No explanation of how death occurred	38
Gangrene or tetanus	Died from the effects of gangrene or tetanus (lock-jaw)	5
Haemorrhage	Died from loss of blood	9
Hanging	Accidentally hung themselves	2
Home / public house	Died at home or in a public house, usually falling down stairs	65
Homicide	Accidental or justifiable homicide	2
Inflammation	Died as a result of inflamed tissues	6
Intoxication	Died where intoxication was the primary cause	37
Manslaughter	Died as a result of another person's activity as pronounced by the coroner – a trial would follow at the Nottingham Assizes	35
Miscarried	Died as a result of a miscarriage	5
Miscellaneous	Died from eating to excess, over-exertion or by fright etc.	6
Murder - known	Killed by a person present at the inquest – a trial would follow at the Nottingham Assizes	23
Murder – unknown	Died as a result of an unknown person or person's activity	21
Natural	Died from natural causes	1898
Opiates	Accidentally died from an overdose of a medicine containing opium	146
Play accident	Children who died whilst at play	17
Poison	Died after accidentally taking or being given a poisonous substance	26
Quarry accident	Died in a quarry usually from a fall of stone or earth	8
Railway accident	Killed on a railway	55
Shooting or stabbing	Accidentally killed by a gun, bow & arrow or a knife	19
Smothered	Died from being accidentally smothered or suffocated	72
Still-birth	Born dead	31
Suicide or felo-de-se	By hanging, drowning, shooting, jumping or taking poison	323
Trampled	Died as a result of being accidentally crushed in a crowd	1
Well accident	Died in a well	19
Windmill accident	Killed at a windmill, usually struck by a sail	11
Workplace accident	Died in a workplace other than a coal-mine, quarry or railway	83
Total number of inquests		**4465**

[a] Sometimes an inquest may have been held on more than one person

1. Accidental overdose of opiates

The practice of giving children sedatives had been prevalent for many years but it became more widespread in the nineteenth century with an increase in the supply of opium from the Mediterranean.[42] It was not unusual therefore to give opiates to children to induce sleep or to control diarrhoea. Working mothers routinely used them when they left their babies in the charge of elderly relatives or other unskilled persons. These child minders would be more willing to agree to this responsibility if the parents provided the necessary '*quieting mixture*' for they only wished to care for an undemanding child.[43] Laudanum (which contained about 40 grains of opium per fluid ounce) was the constituent of two main patent preparations, '*Dalby's Carminative*' or the more notorious '*Godfrey's Cordial*.'[44] These were readily obtained from grocers, corner shopkeepers and chemists in Nottingham and other places in the county. Laudanum was also available, and from this mothers would make-up their own sedative preparation or they might administer it in its undiluted form drop by drop. In 1862 a chemist in Nottingham said that he sold about 400 gallons of laudanum each year and estimated that about half of this was given to children.[45] The overwhelming problem was the variability of the potency of the available opium. The product itself varied between the countries of origin but more importantly the wholesalers, who were only concerned with their profit margins, also adulterated it. This had the disastrous result that the products, when sold over-the-counter, varied widely in strength and it is little wonder that the chance of over-dosing unfortunate children became a reality. After public concern supported by a press that clamoured for government action, a Bill was, after many years of delay, finally published in 1868 restricting the sale of poisons.[46] Opiates were included but only in part II of the Schedule of Poisons and therefore only a registered chemist or druggist or a legally-qualified apothecary could sell them. They also had to be in a container labelled poison with the name of the vendor, but unlike other poisons there was no need to enter them in a register, nor for the buyer to be known or any restriction placed on the amount sold. Also more importantly the Act excluded patent medicines from regulation and no serious attempts were made to discourage the sale of proprietary infant sedatives. At this time it appears that children were not deemed very important, they had no rights, either in the family or out of it. So for many more years the sale of '*Godfrey's Cordial*' etc., went unrestricted. It was not until the Pharmacy Act of 1908 placed opium and all other preparations containing over one per cent morphine into part I of the Schedule of Poisons that there was effective control of the marketing of opiates.

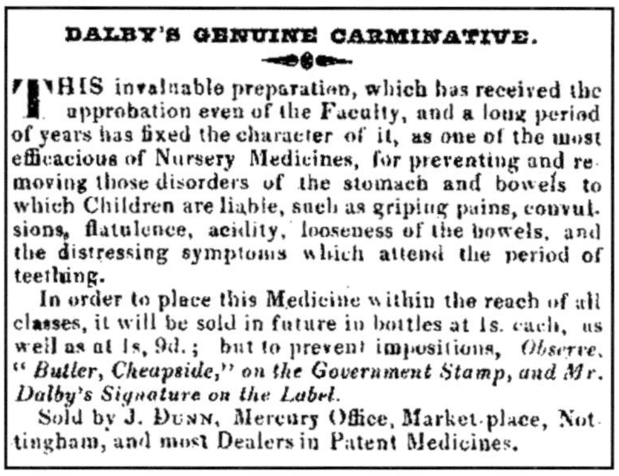

DALBY'S GENUINE CARMINATIVE.

THIS invaluable preparation, which has received the approbation even of the Faculty, and a long period of years has fixed the character of it, as one of the most efficacious of Nursery Medicines, for preventing and removing those disorders of the stomach and bowels to which Children are liable, such as griping pains, convulsions, flatulence, acidity, looseness of the bowels, and the distressing symptoms which attend the period of teething.

In order to place this Medicine within the reach of all classes, it will be sold in future in bottles at 1s. each, as well as at 1s, 9d.; but to prevent impositions, *Observe*, "*Butler, Cheapside*," *on the Government Stamp, and Mr. Dalby's Signature on the Label.*

Sold by J. DUNN, Mercury Office, Market-place, Nottingham, and most Dealers in Patent Medicines.

Advertisement for Dalby's Carminative: a patent medicine prepared with laudanum (1832)

Coroner Swann dealt with many cases in which overdoses of opium were implicated in the cause of death either as the sole cause or as a contributing factor. The majority of these deaths were in children and the patent medicine, '*Godfrey's Cordial*', the main culprit. This was a typical example:

An overdose of '*Godfrey's Cordial*' *'An inquest was held on Thursday 15th August 1833 at the White Lion, Selston, relative to the death of an unbaptised female infant, the bastard child of Elizabeth Cooper, of Brinsley. ... In consequence of the child being restless she bought a pennyworth of 'Godfrey's Cordial' and on Saturday gave it half a tablespoonful; nobody was present and no one had told her how much to give it; it slept well on Sunday and began to have fits on Monday. ... The next morning at ten the child died. She gave three shillings for a coffin but was not able to raise the other shilling to bury it. ... When Mr. Bland the constable asked her if she had given the child anything she at first denied it but later recanted because she was afraid they would open it up. ... The jury returned a verdict that the child died in consequence of too large a dose of 'Godfrey's Cordial' being ignorantly administered by her mother.'*[47]

White Lion, Selston (2001)

Sometimes an inquest was more protracted than in the above case, for there may have been extenuating circumstances that the jury had to take into consideration. It was then their task to determine whether or not the death of a child was due to deliberate or accidental administration of too large a quantity of laudanum. Unless the intent to commit murder could be proved, the mother would be let off with a caution from the coroner. Although they were too young to be sworn, children were sometimes asked to give evidence as illustrated in the inquest detailed below:

An overdose of laudanum *'An inquest was held on Thursday 30th January 1840, at the Beehive, Sneinton, respecting the death of Frances Violetta Lee, aged three weeks. Eliza Pepper being sworn, said that the deceased was the illegitimate child of Julia Lee, she came to lodge at my house three months ago and was confined and delivered of the deceased. On last Tuesday afternoon we were making shirts together when we heard a noise. Julia Lee appeared frightened and said she had given the baby six drops of laudanum and perhaps that was the cause. I went upstairs with my son George and found the child in strong convulsions. The mother followed us and produced a bottle, the colour of the contents resembled that of laudanum, which she emptied into the chamber pot. I took the baby downstairs and I sat with her until midnight. Four doctors had been contacted but they would not come and the baby died on Wednesday morning. Eliza Pepper said that the child was sometimes shaken by the mother and handled roughly whilst she was being dressed. I have heard her call the child a little devil and say "I wish I had a dose of laudanum I'll cure you". This evidence was collaborated by another witness. Two of the children of Eliza Pepper aged 12 and 11 years old were also called to give evidence. The inquest was adjourned for a post-mortem examination. The result of this examination by two doctors was unremarkable but they concluded that six drops of laudanum would be amply sufficient to cause the death of so young an infant. They had not however detected any morphine-like material in the stomach contents. Verdict: That the deceased has been poisoned by an overdose of laudanum being administered to her by her mother but there is not sufficient evidence to satisfy the jury that the mother wilfully intended to destroy the life of her child.'*[48]

Although the majority of deaths ascribed to taking opiates in one form or another were in children, Coroner Swann occasionally held inquests on the bodies of adults whose demise appeared to be caused by an overdose of these products:

An overdose of laudanum by an adult *'An inquest was held on the 21st July 1848 at the sign of the Crown & Woolpack in Sutton-in-Ashfield touching the death of William Saxton aged 45 years. The deceased was a framework knitter and he had been ailing for some time* *but recently he appeared worse than usual. A few days prior to the inquest he was visiting*

his friend, James Marriott, but as he was too ill to return home he stayed overnight. At four o'clock Mr. Marriott heard him breathing very heavily and an hour later he appeared to be dying. Medical help was requested but the surgeon said that little could be done to assist him and he soon died. He had taken laudanum the previous evening to enable him to rest. Verdict: Death from natural causes accelerated by an overdose of laudanum taken by himself to procure rest.'[49]

Crown & Woolpack, Sutton-in-Ashfield (c.1905)

2. Accidental suffocation

In the poorer families, because space in the house was often extremely limited, it was a common practice for very young children to sleep in the same bed with their parents. Indeed other siblings may have also shared this sleeping arrangement. It is therefore not difficult to imagine that the risk of suffocation to babies must have been very great. A coroner's jury had the almost impossible task of trying to determine whether or not suffocation of the young was accidental or deliberate. As in the case of administration of opiates the mother was always given the '*benefit of the doubt*'.

An infant overlain by its drunken mother '*An inquest was held on Friday 13th May 1846 at the Portland Arms, Selston, upon the body of a male infant child of William Frost of Jacksdale-row, blacksmith. The deceased was only 15 days old and not named. According to the mother's statement he was very poorly on the previous Sunday and Monday. She said that during Monday night she gave the infant the breast and it was alive at four o'clock on Tuesday morning, but on awaking an hour afterwards she discovered it was dead and discoloured about the mouth. The inquest was held in consequence of it being reported that Mrs. Frost "had got drunk and overlain the child;" she said most positively that she did not overlay the child in consequence of being intoxicated and that she did not give the child aniseeds in its food. ...Elizabeth Grainy, Mrs. Frost's neighbour, on the contrary declared that on Monday night, she smelt aniseeds in the child's food. She also saw Mrs. Frost on Tuesday morning after the child was dead and thought that she was not very sober. The following note was attached to the inquest:- "The body of the child was extremely black and presented the appearance of having been suffocated by pressure and it is well known in the neighbourhood that the mother is a great drinker and frequently intoxicated and that her evidence was flatly contradicted in all its material parts. The jury were of the opinion that she had no distinct recollection of anything which occurred on Monday night but she had given false evidence and that she fell asleep in her drunkenness and overlaid her child." The jury returned a verdict that the child died in consequence of being accidentally overlain by its mother.'*[50]

Accidental suffocation of a child '*An inquest was held on Tuesday 30th October 1866 at the White Lion, Sneinton, on the body of a child five weeks old, the son of Henry Hinton, a working man. The parents of the deceased lived with Mr. Hinton's father and mother, in Ebenezer Square, Lowdham Street and from the evidence, it appeared that their two children - a girl nearly two years of age and the deceased had been in the habit of sleeping with them. On Sunday night the father and daughter retired early, the mother followed them, with the baby, between eight and nine o'clock. She gave the deceased the breast when in bed and fell asleep while he was feeding and not waking until two next morning when the little girl roused her. That led to the discovery that the baby was dead and a police officer was called in and* *was informed of the occurrence. When found the deceased was lying in the position in which he was placed the previous night, with the nipple still in his mouth and the indications were those of death by suffocation. The jury adopted that view, though the mother was closely examined with respect to giving 'Godfrey's Cordial' to her children, which she admitted. A verdict of accidental death was recorded.'*[51]

3. Accidental burns

Many children lost their lives as a result of serious burns they received primarily from the household fire because they were apt to sit too close to the flames. The smocks worn by children were especially vulnerable and the editor of the Nottingham Review commented: '*That many of these events would not have occurred had a wire fire guard, that valuable article where children assemble and play, been fixed before the fire.*'[52]

The living room of a working class home (1862)

A spark from a fire ignited a little girl's clothes '*An inquest was held on Thursday 12th November 1835 at the Mason's Arms, Bulwell, to inquire into the death of Mary Haslam a little girl under two years of age. She was burnt to death from her clothes taking fire during the absence of her mother on Tuesday morning last, the child had been left about four minutes, playing with her sisters, one aged six, the other eleven. From the evidence of the former the deceased was sitting near the fire when a spark flew out upon her clothes. The neighbours attempted to extinguish the flames but she was so much burnt about the whole of her body that she expired at half past three in the afternoon. Verdict: Accidental death.*'[52]

Mason's Arms, Bulwell (c.1900)

There were also occasions when children died as a result of playing with fire in one form or another:

A young boy received burns at a bonfire '*An inquest was held on Wednesday 17th June 1846, at the Wheat Sheaf, Radford, touching the death of John Hickton, aged seven years. He was burnt to death in consequence of some boys at a bonfire having thrown lighted shavings upon his clothes and set them on fire.* [It seems that it had become the practice for boys to make fires in the neighbourhood of Radford and when they were burning, the bigger boys urged the younger ones to jump over and through the flames. They also throw lighted sticks around to the great annoyance of persons in the vicinity, if anyone interferes he usually meets with abuse from the boys' parents.] *On the present occasion several boys who were engaged in making the fire were brought before the coroner and jury. They endeavoured to establish their own innocence by laying the blame upon the other. It was quite clear, however, that George Merrin was the one that threw fire on the deceased's pinafore, though he stoutly denied the fact. The coroner set the boys at liberty after giving them a severe reprimand. Verdict: Died in consequence of being accidentally burnt.*'[53]

Wheat Sheaf, Radford (1930)

The clothes of a child were set on fire by the flame of a candle *'On Thursday 13th November 1828 an inquest was taken at the Red Lion, Hucknall Torkard, on view of the body of Thomas Norman, aged four years. The deceased and a little girl, his own age, were playing upstairs in the frame-shop in the house of widow Clarke when she heard screaming and running upstairs she found the deceased who was dressed in a cotton frock and trousers enveloped in flames. She endeavoured, but in vain, to extinguish the fire, upon which she ran down the stairs and gave an alarm in the yard. Henry Brown, a neighbour, on coming in, observed something black upstairs and found the deceased lying on the landing-place, on his belly; the flames were not quite extinct but his clothes were nearly all burnt away. He took the child down into the house, where other neighbours stripped off the clothes, and they dressed the wounds with oil. No part of his body was unburned the hair was completely consumed and wherever he was touched the skin came off. The child must have been on fire for nearly ten minutes. He was sensible and when asked how it happened he said "Kitty Oscroft had set him on fire and it was done with a candle" this was his little playmate. He died the same evening at eleven o'clock. Verdict: Accidentally burnt to death.'*[54]

Red Lion, Hucknall (1998)

Sometimes both mother and child died from substantial burns as in the tragic case in Lambley in December 1834:

Robin Hood & Little John, Lambley (1932)

Mother and son burnt to death *'An inquest was held at the Robin Hood & Little John, Lambley, relative to the death of Samuel Culley, aged five months, who was burnt in his cradle which fell into the fire. His mother also received severe burns but she had been taken to Nottingham and died in the General Hospital. The jury returned a verdict of accidental death, at the same time expressing the opinion that the father was highly censurable for leaving his wife alone so long, when he knew she was subject to fits and not capable of taking care of herself.'*[55]

There were a number of disastrous fires resulting from the incautious use of highly flammable materials, which had fatal consequences:

A child received extensive burns when a pan of boiling naphtha caught fire *'An inquest was held on the 15th December 1863 at the Pheasant, Radford touching the death of George Hadden aged 18 months. It appears that the father of the deceased had purchased a small still for the purpose of distilling naphtha. He was boiling a quantity of this naphtha over a fire in the back yard, when a brick fell out of the temporarily constructed fireplace and the pan containing the boiling fluid fell over and ignited everything in the yard. The deceased with his brother, a boy of nine years of age, took refuge in the petty. The father fearing that the fire would consume the place where they stood ran in to fetch them out and as he was re-crossing the yard he stumbled. The younger child fell into the burning substance and before his father, who was also very badly burnt, could rescue him, he was shockingly injured and shortly afterwards he died. In answer to the coroner, the deceased's father said he had sufficient experience in distilling to understand what he was doing. He was doing it to get a little food for his family. Verdict: Death from burning.'*[56]

Pheasant, Radford (1998)

Two sisters received serious burns when a pan of boiling varnish caught fire '*An inquest was held on the 22nd October 1838 at the Nag's Head, East Leake, relative to the death of Ann Richardson, aged 28 years. It appears that the husband of the deceased had been brought up as a gardener but in the summer of this year, had commenced business as a druggist, having previously little experience. He was in the house-place making a varnish, of which the ingredients were: oil, spirits of turpentine, white resin and shellac, all of which are highly combustible substances. They had been in a saucepan, for nearly an hour, when suddenly the varnish caught fire and exploded with a report as loud as a gun. The man was set on fire, as was also his wife's sister, Martha Smith, who was in the house-place at the time. Mrs. Richardson, the deceased, who was in the garden, came running in and met her sister all in flames and was by her set on fire. She then rushed into the house of a neighbour, Mrs. Staples, and in so doing she and her little boy were also burnt. After a few days Ann Richardson died. The jury returned a verdict: Accidental death. A second inquest was held on the 25th October 1838 at the Bull's Head, East Leake, on the body of her sister, Martha Smith, who had died a few days later. The jury returned a similar verdict.*'[57, 58]

Nag's Head, East Leake (1998)

The editor of the Nottingham Mercury commented:

'*The explosion of varnish has been the cause of the most disastrous consequences, beside the two deaths a great many others were also burnt. The husband's arm is burnt in a most dreadful manner and the neighbour, Samaria Staples was also seriously affected. Several other neighbours were also burnt in attempting to extinguish the flames on the sufferers and on the whole we consider this a most dreadful catastrophe.*'[58]

4. Accidental scalds

A large number of children died as a result of a strange practice of drinking hot water out of the spout of a kettle whilst it was on the hob or fire. This had a predictable result if the water happened to be at or near boiling point:

A child drunk boiling water from a kettle spout '*An inquest was held on Tuesday 19th April 1842 at the Magna Charta, Lowdham, to ascertain the cause of death of Elizabeth Herring aged four years. Her mother said that on Friday evening she took the kettle off the fire after it had boiled for tea and placed it on the hob and while getting tea ready, the child drank some water from the spout. She then cried out and she was given some milk, train oil and treacle, when she seemed better, played and went to bed. About two o'clock on Saturday morning the deceased made a rutting noise and her mother sat with her but she gradually got worse and died on Sunday night. Verdict: Died in consequence of being accidentally scalded by drinking boiling water from a tea-kettle.*'[59]

The boiling kettle: a hazard to children (1844)

Death from drinking boiling water out of a tea-kettle *'An inquest was held on the 24th March 1845 at the Barley Mow, Basford on the body of Samuel Brown, two years old, the son of a framework knitter living at Parson's Flat. It appears that the child's mother was sitting at a table resting her head upon her hand. The child, unobserved by her, drank some boiling water out of a tea-kettle, which was upon the hob, and unfortunately so low that the deceased could reach the spout. The mother had only recently had the kettle and the child had never been allowed to drink out of it. Mr. Radcliffe, surgeon, was requested to visit, but after lingering until the afternoon of the following day death put an end to the child's sufferings. Verdict: Death from being accidentally scalded by drinking boiling water from a tea-kettle.'*[60]

The editor of the Nottingham Review commented:

'Amongst the poor the habit of allowing children to drink out of the kettle spout is not uncommon. It is a foolish and filthy practice to say the least of it and seeing such dreadful accidents that may occasionally result we trust it will be a warning to some of our readers.'[52]

The Review was obviously correct but its comments were unlikely to have been communicated to the homes in which this practice was prevalent. Over the years Christopher Swann continued to preside, from time to time, at inquests where children had died as a result of this type of scalding accident. One of his last occasions was on Christmas Day 1865 (page 22).

5. Accidental choking

There were a number of fatalities where a child was choked to death by food or foreign substances that had lodged in his or her throat. On occasions unqualified persons attempted inappropriate treatment or had tried to extract these objects only to make the situation worse by forcing them down into the trachea:

A nutshell becomes lodged in a child's throat *'An inquest was held on Tuesday 17th October 1843 at the New Inn, Carrington, to ascertain the cause of death of Elizabeth Woodward. A few weeks ago, a piece of nutshell lodged in this child's throat. Being ill from inflammation a Mr. Caunt, druggist, living in the neighbourhood was called in ... he treated the child for inflammation of the lungs, by leeching, and a warm bath. This was on Monday evening, the 9th October; up to Friday of that week the child kept getting worse and mustard plasters were applied. Mr. Thompson was called in on that day, on examination he said the complaint lay in the windpipe, but he would not give a farthing for the child's life. If it would be of any satisfaction to the mother he would send it some medicine. The child died next morning. On post-mortem examination Mr. Thompson found the lungs quite healthy but in the windpipe and larynx a great deal of inflammation caused by portions of lodged nutshell. Verdict: Died from inflammation and suffocation, in consequence of the accidental lodgement of a bit of nut or chestnut shell in the larynx. The jury is of the opinion that William Caunt is highly censurable for not giving the case to a regular medical man.'*[61]

White Lion, Lowdham (c.1920)

A piece of apple becomes lodged in a child's throat *'An inquest was held on the 29th August 1850, at the White Lion, Lowdham over the body of George Chapman, aged 15 months. On the previous morning the mother gave the deceased a little piece of apple but a short time later he started to cry and the little girl who nursed him took him back to his mother. However, the little boy turned black in the face, struggled and* *died in a few minutes. Verdict: That the deceased died in a sudden fit of passion but whether he was accidentally choked on the piece of apple or not no evidence appears to prove.'*[62]

A piece of turnip becomes lodged in a child's throat '*An inquest was held on Monday 8th April 1839 at the New Inn, Lenton, on view of the body of Reubin Abell, 15 months old. On Saturday three weeks ago, while eating some turnips, he choked; the mother took the child to Mr. Mortimer, druggist, who forced the turnip down the child's throat by means of his own finger. The child had three fits, was put into a warm bath and had some powders given to it. On Sunday it had a fourth fit and was taken to Mr. Mortimer who put it in a warm bath and tried to bleed it with a lancet in the arm but no blood came. The child died in the water. Verdict: Death from natural causes.'*[63]

Henry C. Attenburrow, Honorary Secretary to the British Medical Association, castigated the activities of Mr. Mortimer and by implication the inquest verdict of '*natural causes'*. Writing in the local press he said: '*Surely this was a case for medical investigation, were it only for the purpose of protecting the public against the mischievous interference of ignorant and irregular practitioners.'*[15]

6. Accidents on the road

There were many accidents that occurred on the roads of the county. These fell into two groups, firstly - deaths of pedestrians, usually children, being knocked down or run over by carts or occasionally stagecoaches. Secondly – deaths of persons who fell from moving vehicles and were run over. Many of these latter accidents occurred as a result of the risky practice of the driver sitting on the shafts of a cart or allowing children to ride in that dangerous position:

A child is crushed by a horse and cart '*An inquest was held on Monday 6th June 1842 at the house of Isaac Mosley, retail beer seller, Radford, relative to the death of Eliza Hind. On the previous Friday, the deceased, who was the daughter of John Hind, lacemaker, Radford, went out of her father's house and stood by the river Leen, opposite to her house. While looking at some children playing, a mare and cart, driven by a lad, came along the road, when the animal suddenly turned round to drink in the river. One of the wheels of the cart caught the child, threw her down crushing her head against a corner-stone of a wall. She died in the evening of the next day from the injuries so received. Verdict: Died in consequence of being accidentally run over by a mare and cart, the property of William Leadbetter of Ilkeston, coal-higgler; and the jury imposed a deodand of £5 on the mare and cart.'*[64]

A young boy is run over by the Times stagecoach '*An inquest was held on Sunday 27th January 1833 at the Horse & Jockey, Stapleford relative to the death of Thomas Bramley, aged nearly five years. The little boy was playing on the turnpike road, in front of his father's house, when the Times coach from Nottingham to Derby was coming down the hill. The coachman called out to him and the little boy attempted to cross the road but was knocked down by the leader. The driver succeeded in pulling up before the wheel reached the child but he was severely injured by the horse's hooves and he died within the hour. ... It appeared that the road was being repaired and a bank had been left two feet high and being frightened he ran back again and was trodden on by the horses. ... Verdict: Accidental death with a recommendation that the*

Stagecoach (1843)

surveyor of highways should immediately cause the dirt and rubbish by the side of the road to be removed and the causeway lowered and put into a complete state of repair.'[65] [The slate headstone, in memory of Thomas Bramley, survives and may be seen, with its long poignant epitaph, in the graveyard of the parish church in Stapleford.]

Danger of riding on shafts – a comment by the Nottingham Journal in 1835 reads:

'*We have frequently had occasion to notice the dangerous practice of riding on the shafts and we have this week the painful duty of recording another fatal accident resulting from this practice*'. One such incident occurred in Oxton some years later:

A young boy fell from the shafts of a cart '*An inquest was held on Monday the 4th July 1847 at the Bridge House,* [renamed the Olde Bridge Inn in 1929] *Oxton, upon Thomas Paulson, four years old, the illegitimate child of Maria Paulson, of Radford. It appears from the evidence of John Burton, of Oxton, cottager, that on Saturday afternoon he was loading clover in his waggon and took his nephew, a child, and the deceased for a ride. He placed his nephew on the fore horse and the deceased on the shafts of the waggon and in this manner the children rode twice from the field. Burton went a third time to the field and again placed his nephew on the fore horse and the deceased on the shafts of the waggon telling him to hold fast; Burton walking by the side of his horses. When they had come about three quarters of a mile, he turned his head from the deceased to knock a fly off which was biting the horse, when the deceased fell off the shafts and the wheels passed over the child's head and killed him. The coroner addressed Burton upon his thoughtless conduct in placing a young child upon the shafts and expressed regret that in consequence of the law of deodands being repealed he could not impose a fine. Burton, who appeared much distressed, said that he would never be guilty of such folly again. The jury returned the following verdict: Accidentally killed by being run over by a waggon.'*[66]

Bridge Inn, Oxton (1997)

Another young boy fell from a cart '*An inquest was held on the 24th April 1854 at the Nag's Head, Kirkby-in-Ashfield on the body of Edward Harpham aged 12 years. Two days earlier William Hayes was driving a drug laden with timber on the road from Blidworth to Pinxton when Edward Harpham who had been walking along the road, got on to the cart and sat on a pole which projected behind the wheels. He had ignored the advice of the driver who told him that this was a dangerous practice. Unfortunately as the cart was going down the hill into Kirkby he fell off and the wheels passed over his head and body. He lay motionless on the ground and was found to be dead. The jury returned a verdict that he was accidentally killed in consequence of being run over.'*[67]

Nag's Head, Kirkby-in-Ashfield (1960)

7. Accidents on the farm

There were a number of fatal accidents on farms that were brought to the attention of Coroner Swann. Many of these involved falls from haystacks or from carts loaded with hay or falls from trees:

A farm worker fell from a cart on to his hay-fork '*An inquest was held on the 31st August 1850, at the Red Lion, Ruddington, over the body of William Murden. The deceased was a labourer, 38 years old. He and another man were engaged in loading a waggon with straw and when they had got a full load, the deceased stuck his fork into the straw and rested with his arms leaning on top of the shaft. ... As the waggon moved off half the load fell off and the deceased came down with it and fell on to his fork in such a manner that the grains entered his right breast. ... Blood and foam came from his mouth and he was carried home but he died in two or three minutes after he entered the house. ... Verdict: Accidental death.*'[68]

A young woman fell from a haystack on to a thatch peg '*An inquest was held at the Commercial Inn, Beeston, on the 27th August 1854 on the body of Hannah Cherry, aged 21 years. The deceased was a servant of Mr. Radford, farmer of Beeston Fields, and was in the habit of going into the stack-yard to look for eggs...On Saturday about a quarter to eight she proceeded on that errand. She had been gone about 20 minutes when her master called her to draw some beer for the harvest people but could not make her hear. A search was made for her and she was found lying quite dead at the foot of a straw stack. She was carried into the house and Mr. Orton, surgeon, was promptly fetched. On examining her person, a thatch peg was discovered to have penetrated her body as far as 18 inches. The terrible accident was then explained. She must have reared the ladder against the stack and ascended to search for eggs but on stepping on a sheaf of straw it gave way. She was then precipitated to the earth and fell upon a thatch peg that penetrated her private parts, passed through the vagina and pierced her body where it broke. Of course death was instantaneous. ... A verdict was returned in accordance with the above fact.*'[69]

Commercial Inn, Beeston (1998)

Although some mechanisation was gradually being introduced on to farms in the county, primarily for threshing corn, there were very few deaths reported to the coroner involving these machines; one of these rare events is described below:

A boy became entangled in a corn-threshing machine '*An inquest was held on Friday 15th September 1848 at the Denman's Head, Sutton-in-Ashfield, to inquire into the death of William Peach, aged about nine years old. Joseph Allwood had a corn-threshing machine on his farm and the deceased and several others went into the stack-yard to watch the machine working. ... The boy came too close to the machine the spindle of which was caught in his smock and he got drawn up into the mechanism. The horses were immediately stopped but the boy must have been turned round with the rapidly revolving spindle but he was already dead by the time he was extricated, his forehead was cut to pieces and his left leg broken from which a bone protruded. The spindle had no box or cover over it but the farmer said that he had hired the machine on several occasions but they had never had an accident with it before. A witness said that if the spindle had been boxed-in this accident would not have occurred. Verdict: Accidentally killed by a corn-threshing machine.*'[70]

Denman's Head, Sutton-in-Ashfield (1997)

8. Accidentally killed by an animal

The horse was the most common animal that was in close association with humans so it is therefore not surprising that the greatest number of fatal incidents was associated with this creature. The accidents were generally ascribed to being kicked or to injuries sustained following a fall from horseback. A few other deaths were reported due to being gored by bulls or cows and to a lesser extent subsequent to having been bitten by a dog:

A young boy was kicked by a horse in a field '*An inquest was held on the 8th August 1834, at the Jolly Colliers, Kirkby-in-Ashfield, on view of the body of William Hunt, aged about two years. ... It appears that the deceased was playing on Selston Common, where there were five horses grazing and the child stood about a yard and a half from one of them. The animal advanced and struck him down with one of its fore legs and twice jumped over the deceased and smelt the blood that had flowed from the head of the child. The horse was with difficulty driven away and upon the deceased being lifted up it continued stamping and pawing the ground. The back part of the head of the child was much bruised and a portion of his brains lay upon the Common. Verdict: Accidental death with a deodand of ten shillings upon the horse.*'[71]

Another accident involving a horse '*An inquest was held on the 3rd October 1851 at the Lord Nelson, Burton Joyce, on the body of John Clayton, aged 13, a servant in the employ of Richard Thorpe, landlord of the above public house. On Wednesday 1st October, about six o'clock in the evening, the deceased was endeavouring to catch a pony that had strayed into a croft near his master's house when the animal suddenly turned round and kicked him in the stomach. ... The boy was taken home and Mr. Osbourne, surgeon called in, but he thought the boy was in no great danger, however, proper medicines were administered. The boy seemed to be recovering until the following morning when he got up and drank a quantity of cold sour ale. Shortly afterwards he complained of feeling much worse and Mr. Osbourne was again sent for but Clayton expired the same evening. Verdict: Died from the injuries that he received by being accidentally kicked by a pony.*'[72]

Lord Nelson, Burton Joyce (c.1870)

A man is gored by a cow '*An inquest was held on the 24th May 1843 at the house of William Spittal, farmer, Widmerpool, relative to the death of John Spittal, father of the above, aged 83. On Saturday, the deceased walked out with Thomas Barnett, to fetch in the cows and while the deceased stood at the gate, holding it open, one of the cows instead of quietly passing through, ran at him. He was gored so seriously that he died from his injuries on Sunday about half past one. Verdict: Died from injuries he received by being gored by a cow, the property of Thomas Barnett of Widmerpool Cottage, with a deodand of five pounds on the cow.*'[73]

A girl is bitten by a dog '*An inquest was held on Sunday 17th June 1832 at the General Hospital, Nottingham, before Christopher Swann, relative to the death of Jane Morris Watson, aged 13 years. On Wednesday prior to her death she was bitten by a stray dog, the wound however soon healed but she later started to feel ill. ... Apparently the boys in the village began to taunt her and called after her "Jane you'll go mad" and other expressions that worried her. She was taken to the Hospital in Nottingham but her condition got worse and the sight of fluids caused her to be convulsed. ... After having been bled and other remedies applied she died. The jury returned a verdict of hydrophobia and strongly censured the unfeeling conduct of boys in taunting the deceased as they did.*'[74]

9. Died after accidental poisoning

Poisonous substances were readily obtained from druggists in Nottingham throughout the period of Swann's career as a coroner. Many of the more dangerous ones were sold with little more precaution than the simplest preparations. In a letter to the Nottingham Review in 1844 Michael Browne, the Coroner for Nottingham, expressed his concern that druggists often sold arsenic to children more frequently than to adults.[75] It was not until the Pharmacy Act of 1868 that any statutory regulation of their sale to the public was implemented. Fatal accidents occurred for a number of reasons, sometimes substances were simply taken or given to a child in mistake for less innocuous preparations or the wrong product was sold by the druggist. On other occasions children ate materials left out for other purposes; for example those items which were intended to be used as an adult medicine or as a poison for rats, mice or flies. Also death occurred after an unintentional drug overdose. These accidents are illustrated by a cross-section of inquests:

A child was given sulphuric acid in mistake for laudanum *'An inquest was held on Monday 18th April 1836 at the Plough* [renamed World's End in 1973], *Lowdham, on the body of John Allcock, aged four months. It appears that his mother routinely gave the child 'Godfrey's Cordial' (laudanum), and finding that she did not have a supply she went to her uncle in order to borrow some. Unfortunately neither her uncle nor her aunt were at home and their daughter aged about 11 years gave her oil of vitriol* [sulphuric acid] *by mistake, which her father used for making blacking. The mother of the deceased poured out half a teaspoonful and on placing it to the lips of the child, he screamed out and pushed the spoon away. A surgeon was sent for but the little boy died at two o'clock the next morning. Verdict: Accidental death.'*[76]

Plough Inn, Lowdham (c.1960)

A vendor of drugs cautioned by the coroner for not labelling her products *'An inquest was held on Monday 22nd January 1864 at the Moulder's Arms, Radford, on the body of a female child five days old. The child had not had good health and her mother, Mrs. Bull, had obtained some ipecacuhana wine and she administered five drops that appeared to improve the child's breathing. The following morning with the intention of giving the child another dose she took a bottle from the side-board and administered five drops out of it. However, she was soon alerted to the fact that she had by mistake given the child laudanum; apparently she had been taking this during her confinement. Medical help was immediately obtained but remedies were of no avail and the child died three to four hours later. The colour of both liquids was similar and one might be easily mistaken for the other. Mrs. Stevenson, a vendor of drugs in Radford, said she sold laudanum to Mrs. Bull and said she did not label the bottle. The coroner cautioned her that she was liable to a heavy penalty for selling drugs without labelling the bottles. Verdict: That the child died from the effects of an overdose of laudanum administered by mistake.'*[77]

A druggist's assistant prepared a medicine with laudanum instead of paregoric *'An inquest was held on Wednesday 27th April 1836 at the Unicorn, Sutton-in-Ashfield, touching the death of Alan Witham, aged three months. His mother had requested Mr. Littlewood, druggist, to supply her with a mixture of syrup of rhubarb, syrup of violets, paregoric and honey. It appears that his assistant, Tristram Poundall, put a drachm of laudanum in it instead of paregoric, the bottles standing by the side of each other on the shelf. The apprentice denied most positively having made any mistake, but analysis of the mixture* *proved Poundall having by mistake sold a portion of laudanum instead of paregoric and therefore laudanum was accidentally administered to the deceased and the jury are of the opinion that he is very blameable.*'[78]

A little girl eats a mixture containing arsenic intended for killing flies '*An inquest was held on Sunday 19th June 1864 at the house of Mr. Braithwaite, East Leake, on the body of his daughter, aged three years six months. On the previous day the little girl was in the cheese-room/kitchen at the farm when she sighted a mixture of sugar mastic and arsenic in a saucer on a shelf, which had been placed there for the purpose of killing flies. She licked some of this mixture which being mostly composed of sugar, was pleasant to the taste and in consequence she was soon seized with violent pains and retching. Medical assistance was obtained as speedily as possible but to no avail and she died after enduring great suffering. She was much beloved by all about the farm and her death has plunged her parents into uncontrollable grief. Verdict: According to the facts.*'[79]

An overdose of colchicum used for treating rheumatic complaints '*An inquest was held at the Old Spot, Arnold, on Saturday 7th October 1848, on the body of Sarah Whitt, aged 40 years. Her husband, David Whitt said that for some time she had suffered from rheumatism, although she had been under the care of Mr. Allen, surgeon, but she had been advised by some neighbours to take tincture of colchicum. Unknown to Mr. Allen she obtained this product and last Monday about five o'clock she took the first dose of half a teaspoonful and at six o'clock took double the quantity. At about seven o'clock she took another teaspoonful and between eight and nine she took the remainder which was nearly two teaspoonfuls. About two o'clock on Tuesday morning she began to vomit and other unfavourable symptoms occurred. Early on Wednesday morning she said she felt very poorly and later when her husband awoke she had died. Mr. Allen said that in his opinion one teaspoonful would have killed her and the quantity she took would have killed a strong healthy person. The jury returned a verdict that the deceased died from the effects of over-doses of colchicum, administered with no evil intent.*'[80] [A medicinal product, colchicine, is still available today for the treatment of acute gout.]

10. Accidentally drowned

The rivers, streams and the canals that crossed Nottinghamshire were a potential hazard, particularly to children, and large numbers of deaths from drowning in these waters were reported to the coroner. The waterways of the Trent, Leen and Soar were scenes of many fatalities and the newspapers were constantly highlighting the dangers of swimming in the Trent; nevertheless it was indeed a popular pastime. Others drowned in lakes, mill-ponds, dykes, springs, or reservoirs. The circumstances surrounding the deaths were varied, some died whilst swimming, others fell from boats, ferries or bridges, whilst others dropped through the ice on canals or mill ponds and some infants perished after falling into water-filled vessels (cisterns, pipkins or dolly-tubs) at home:

A section of the Nottingham canal (1859)

A man found drowned in a sunken boat '*An inquest was held on Sunday 3rd August 1834 at the Fox & Crown, Holme Lane, Holme Pierrepont, on view of the body of William Hutchinson aged 30 years. The deceased was employed by the Trent Navigation Company*

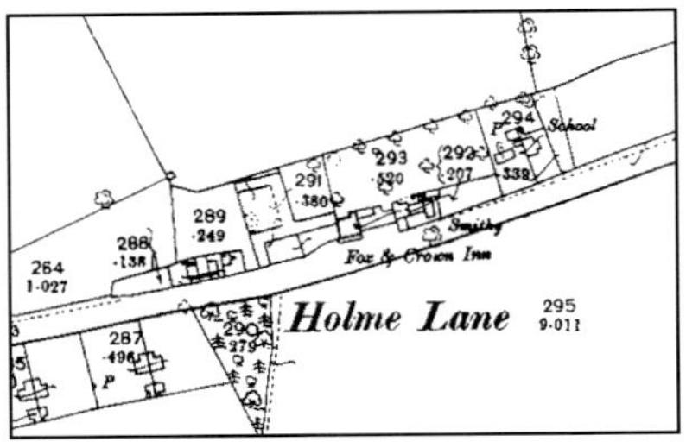

Site of the Fox & Crown, Holme Lane (1884)

and with another man named William Raynor worked on the same boat, getting gravel out of the river Trent at Holme Pierrepont. On Friday night Raynor went to his own house to sleep and left Hutchinson in the boat moored in the Holme canal. At four o'clock on Saturday morning, Raynor found that the boat had sunk and that it was completely under the water. He and several other boatmen ran the water off and opened one of the cabin doors and a man put his hand in and felt the arm of the deceased reared up against the door on the inside. He was then carried out of the cabin and brought into a stable but he was quite dead. The deceased had evidently made an attempt to get out as he lay against the door and not on the bed. One of the cabin doors was fastened and the other closed. The boat was very leaky and wanted repairing but had not been repaired for twelve months. The boat lay in the same place the previous night but now was heavily laden with gravel and this caused it to sink. Verdict: Accidental death with a deodand of 5s. on the boat.'[81]

Two young men fell from a boat on the river Trent '*Two inquests were held, the first on Wednesday 30*th *March 1842 at the Punch Bowl* [later the Ferry Inn], *Wilford, on the body of John Lowater. The second inquest was at the Trent Bridge Inn, West Bridgford on the 9*th *April 1842 on the body of Henry Taylor. It appears that three young friends hired a boat and went on an excursion on the river Trent on Monday the 28*th *March, but as they approached the Wilford Ferry the boat capsized. It appears that a flagpole on the boat may have caught the chain by which the ferryboat is hauled across the river. The young men found themselves in the river and attempts to right the upturned boat failed. Only the third member of the group, James Shaw, managed with the help of a man who was fishing, to reach the bank of the river. Attempts by the ferryman to rescue the others failed and the river was dragged for their bodies and the next day that of John Lowater was found and taken to Wilford Church. The body of Henry Taylor was found by two boys, on the south-side of the Trent near the outflow of the Grantham Canal and taken to the stable of the Trent Bridge Inn. The verdicts of the juries were: Accidentally drowned.*'[82, 83]

Ferry Inn, Wilford (1922)

A man was drowned in the river Trent as he was about to baptise a woman '*An inquest was held on the 11*th *March 1852 at the Jolly Angler, Beeston, to inquire into the death of William Barnes, aged 25 years. A meeting of the Latter Day Saints was held on the evening of the 29*th *January, after which a group of members lead by William Barnes went to Beeston Rylands to baptise a woman, who was to be received into the church. They proceeded to the swing bridge at Trent Lock and walked up to the bottom pier head. The moon was overcast, the wind very rough and the river high with a flood. Barnes went into the water with his arms folded but he fell off the lock wall. He remained for a little time with his head and shoulders above the water but then he floated to the middle of the river. He shouted to be got out but all attempts to save him were to no avail and he was not seen again that night. His decomposed body was not recovered until 11*th *March from just below Clifton Weir, only about 500 yards from where he disappeared. The inquest was held on the same day and the jury returned a verdict that he was accidentally drowned in the river Trent.*'[84]

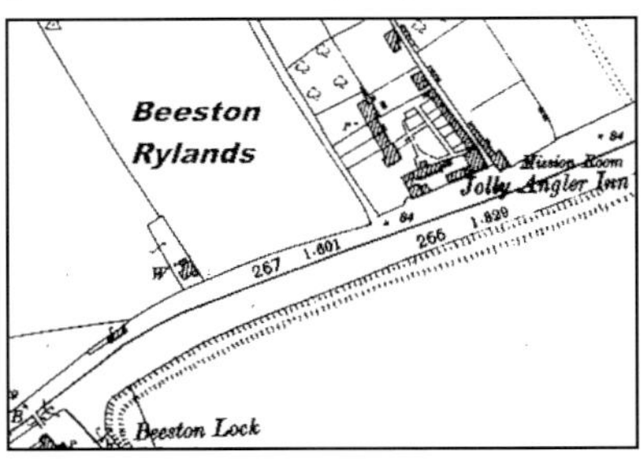

Site of the Jolly Angler, Beeston (1901)

The tragic death of a little girl who drowned in the river Leen '*An inquest was held on the 10th October 1837 at the White Hart, Lenton, on the body of Hannah Kirkham, aged two years two months. George Morris, engineer, Lenton, deposed as follows: Yesterday afternoon about half past one o'clock as I was returning home from Nottingham by the Leen-side, I observed a child floating down the stream under the water. I fetched it out and took it to the Grove Tavern public house, only a few yards distant but William Kitchen who manages the house for Mr. Galtree, the landlord, would not let me put her down. He told the mill-wright who was with me, who had the child in his arms, to take it away. I then tried to get it into the first house I came to below the Grove Tavern, but the woman refused to let us bring it in. I then inquired and found out whose child it was and carried it home but neither the mother nor the father was in. I left it at John Lowe's their next door neighbour, Mrs Lowe wrapped it in a great coat and laid it on the hearth-stone; I then left. The child was alive when I took it out of the water, as I saw it twice open its mouth and move one of its arms. She died whilst we were trying to get it into the house near the Grove Tavern. I think 10 minutes elapsed from the time I took her out of the water to the time she died. The child had been left in the care of the person who lodges with the deceased's parents for the day, as they were gone out to work. Verdict: Accidentally drowned.*'[85]

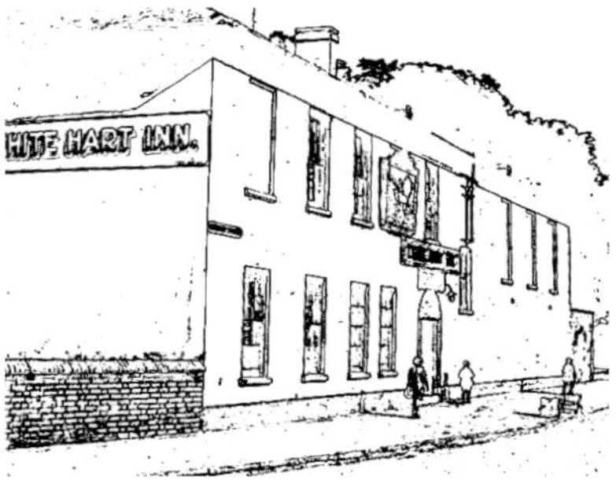

White Hart, Lenton (1930)

A boy was drowned after falling into a lock on the Nottingham canal '*An inquest was held on the 15th May 1845 at the Admiral Rodney, Wollaton to ascertain the cause of death of Israel Knightley. The deceased and three other youths went out the previous day searching for birds' nests. As they were crossing over the lock gates of number 12 lock on the Nottingham canal the deceased struck his foot on a stump near the gate and he fell head first into the water where he was drowned. Verdict: Accidentally drowned.*'[86]

Admiral Rodney, Wollaton (c.1910)

A little girl was drowned in a mill-pond '*An inquest was held on the 31st May 1834 at the Cross Keys, Epperstone, relative to the death of Mary Ann Jallands, aged three years six months. It appeared that the father of the deceased worked at Mr. Foster's paper mill and was raking some weeds out of the mill-dam when he saw the child. He held it up by the heels to let the water run out of it supposing that to be the proper course.* [The Review commented "If there are any remains of life it is sure to destroy them."] *The child had been seen in the mill about 15 minutes ago. The road was by the waterside and there is no fence to prevent people from falling in. Verdict: Accidental death.*'[87]

Cross Keys, Epperstone (1998)

11. Accidental deaths in coal-mines

Numerous deaths, many of which were of boys, occurred in the Nottinghamshire coal-fields. The most commonly reported verdict at a coroner's inquest was that death was the result of a collapse of the roof of the mine. Other tragedies that happened were bodily injury caused by the explosion of gas or

View of a coal-mine (1843)

suffocation from poisonous gas. The three main gases in coal-mines are firedamp, blackdamp and afterdamp. The chief constituent of firedamp is methane produced from decaying vegetable material when the coal-seams were laid down. Methane is very inflammable and when mixed with air produces an easily ignited and explosive mixture. Blackdamp is an inert mixture of nitrogen and carbon dioxide formed by the oxidation of coal and when present in sufficient quantities would be a threat to miners working in poorly ventilated mines. Afterdamp is colourless and odourless and because it contains a high proportion of carbon monoxide is highly poisonous. It is produced from incomplete combustion and is invariably found in mines after an underground fire or explosion.

Other accidents resulted from mechanical failure or from human error when lowering or raising miners in the pit shaft. Before the invention of the cage to transport the men, the asses, coal and all the other attendant materials for working the mine, a crude system of chains and rope was employed. Groups of miners [bantles] would hang on to these chains and the asses would also be tethered to them. Extracted coal was brought out by this means in hazel-wood baskets, known as corves.

During his period in office Christopher Swann presided over numerous inquests as a consequence of deaths in coal-mining accidents and a few of these are highlighted:

Royal Oak, Watnall (1998)

Death of a boy aged nine by a roof fall '*An inquest was held on Tuesday 20th August 1833 at the Royal Oak, Watnall, relative to the death of Edmund Varley, aged nine years. The deceased was employed to drive an ass in a coal-pit, belonging to Messrs. Barber, Walker & Co. and on Friday afternoon, whilst so doing, there was a fall of bind* [indurated clay occurring between coal-strata] *from the roof of the pit, which buried him and the ass. He was got out within five minutes but it was found that he was crushed about the lower parts of his body. It appeared that every precaution had been taken to prevent such an accident, which however, cannot at all times be avoided. He languished until Sunday and then died. Verdict: Accidental death.*'[88]

Colliery explosion of firedamp – two lives lost '*The adjourned inquest was held on Friday 16th December 1864 at the Jolly Colliers, Kimberley, on the bodies of Thomas Davis and Abraham Brown aged 17 years. ...The Government Inspector of Mines was present but the jury objected to the representatives of the Messrs. Barber and Walker's coal-mines being in attendance and they agreed to retire. Samuel Robinson, 14 years old, then deposed – I was working in the pit on the day of the accident and I saw the deceased men near me. Whilst we were working Joel Walters began to buffet the gas with his waistcoat and in a short time the explosion took place. He was driving the gas towards the place where we were working. We were all using naked candles. There were Davy-lamps available but they were not used. The explosion knocked me down and burnt me. I got up immediately. I did not see where the other men were, everything being in darkness but I groped my way to the main road where the lights were still on. I knew that gas was escaping in the pit that morning and that we ought to be careful. I have never read or heard or seen the rules of the pit.... Coroner Swann said that rule 31 says that the under reviewer* [under manager] *or his deputy must see that lock safety lamps are used in all roads wherever firedamp is apprehended. ...The Government Inspector said that the rules state that the gas ought to have been taken out before the men entered the pit.* [This was a long and detailed enquiry and much of the evidence was taken with a view to determining whether anyone was responsible for the accident and it is perhaps ironical that it was held at the Jolly Colliers public house.] *The jury returned a verdict of accidental death.'*[89]

Death through an explosion of gas in a coal-pit *'An inquest was held on the 16th March 1866 at the Half Moon, Hucknall Torkard, into the circumstances attending the death of Edward Kean. He had met his death by an explosion of gas in a pit belonging to the Hucknall Colliery Company. The inquest had been adjourned three times, once in order to give notice to the Inspector of Mines and twice on account of the illness of two jurymen. The deceased was employed in the colliery as a "butty"*[a sub-contractor] *and on Wednesday 17th January was engaged in removing some back timber with the light of a common oil and wick lamp; there were others working with naked candles. He proceeded to knock a bar out, which loosened the bind* [indurated clay occurring between coal-strata] *and caused gas to escape, when some of his fellow-workmen had told him not to or they would be killed. He however persisted in doing this and was lifting up his lantern when gas exploded blowing out all the lights and enveloping the deceased in flames. Other miners were also badly burnt but with the deceased managed to crawl to the pit shaft and then got out. The Deputy Overlooker had properly examined the works in the morning when there was no danger. The deceased had no right to meddle with the bar. ...The jury returned a verdict that the deceased died from the accidental explosion of gas in a coal-pit.'*[90]

Half Moon, Hucknall (1998)

Two men and a boy killed in a coal-pit accident *'An inquest was held on the 24th June 1837 at the Anchor, Skegby near Mansfield, on the bodies of Edward Buxton, aged 41 years, John Gelsthorpe, aged 31 years and Samuel Gelsthorpe, aged eight years. John Buxton, collier, after having been sworn, stated that on Friday morning the 23rd June, at about six o'clock the deceased had fastened themselves in the chains, as usual, after having tackled two asses to the rope and were proceeding down the pit, belonging to John Dodsley. When they had been lowered about 26 yards, I perceived that the rope had broken and heard the colliers scream out. I ran for another rope and put it on and we took the deceased out as quickly as we could. There were several men and boys in the pit at the time. We sent some boxes and straw down and the men below placed the deceased in the box, in which they were drawn up. The asses were sent up first. Both the asses and the two men and the boy were quite dead. My brother had his back broken, neck dislocated and his head was nearly cut off and his legs were broken. The deceased boy had one leg cut off and one nearly so, his head, face and jaws were very much crushed and his teeth were knocked out. John Gelsthorpe's leg was broken and his face much injured. One of the iron caps fastened to the rope broke and let the bolt slip through and the deceased consequently fell to the bottom of the pit, which is 100 yards and two feet deep. They had fallen about 74 yards. I had looked at the rope and caps the night before but I did not see anything amiss with them. I have examined them since and perceived that there was a fault in the welding of the iron in one of the caps and it broke at this point. There is no person appointed whose duty it is to*

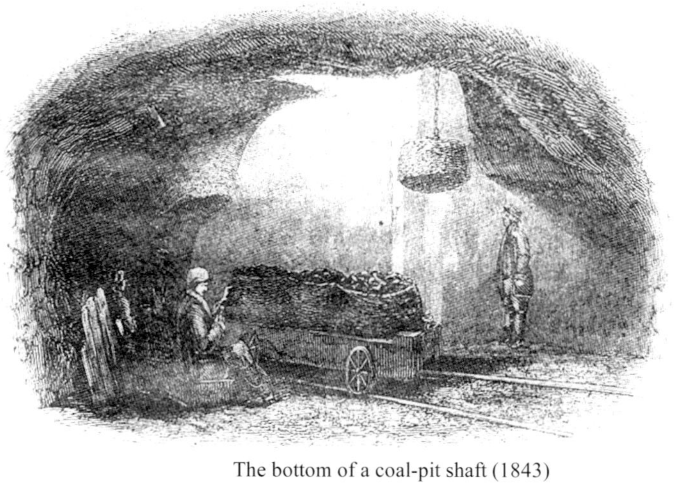

The bottom of a coal-pit shaft (1843)

examine the state of the machinery. All caps ought to be made out of solid iron so as to be perfectly safe, but the cap that broke had been welded and was not so thick as the other caps. [Four men and an ass had gone down a short time previously. As the deceased went down the pit, they were placed in the chains, under the asses, and above them was an iron "umbrella". The umbrella falling upon the deceased was the cause of them being so shockingly mutilated.]. Verdict: Accidental death.'[91]

Two men die in a coal-pit accident through human error '*An inquest was held at the Gate Tavern, Awsworth on the 14th August 1838 and by adjournment on the 16th August at the Lord Nelson, Kimberley, relative to the death of John Siddon, aged 40 years and William Fisher, aged 28 years. They had been killed at Messrs. North & Wakefield's colliery on the previous Monday. It appears from the evidence, that about half past ten in the morning the two men were ascending out of the pit in the chains, when about half way up the shaft the whimsey* [winding engine] *stopped, but in a little while it started again. However, instead of stopping when level with the pit bank the chain continued to revolve and the men were drawn over the wheel and thence dashed to the ground. They sustained severe head injuries from which, later that day, they died. In regard to the cause of the accident, Sampson Chambers, the whimsey boy, stated that he was 14 years old and that his father had been transferred to take charge of the whimsey at another colliery. The boy had then been left in sole charge since Easter but he had never had an accident before. On the morning in question, he found that the whimsey had stopped for want of steam, he then went into the engine house to mend the fire. On his return, a collier named Wheelacre, started the whimsey again and endeavoured to take the hand-iron out of his hands. He said that during this time and from the stopping of the whimsey he did not observe the men when they got to the level of the pit bank, nor did he see them on the wheel. In consequence of what the colliers said to him he was frightened and had run away. The man, Wheelacre, denied being in the whimsey-house* [engine house] *at all but two other colliers confirmed seeing him leaving it at the time of the accident. Several witnesses expressed their opinion that the boy, Chambers, was too young to have charge of the whimsey. The jury returned a verdict of accidental death and in each instance levied a deodand of £15 on the machinery of Messrs. North & Wakefield.'*[92]

Miners descending into a mine by clinging to a chain (1843)

12. Accidental deaths in factories and some other workplaces

Interior of a power-loom factory (1844)

The increase of mechanisation and the rise in the number of factories in the urban areas of Nottinghamshire was accompanied by a commensurate number of fatal accidents. Many of these were the result of operatives, many of them children, becoming entangled or caught-up in unguarded machinery. Other reported deaths were the result of falls from ladders, roofs or scaffolding. Some men were killed by falls of sand, earth or walls in their workplace or suffocated by gas:

A young boy becomes entangled in machinery at a bleach works '*An inquest was held on the 18th September 1846, at the Vernon Arms, Basford, to ascertain the death of Samuel Oxspring. Henry Burton of Basford, aged nine years, said – I knew Samuel Oxspring; he worked at Mr. Cox's Bleach Works, where I work, we were both employed in brushing shirts and hose; the brushes are turned by the steam engine. We were at work yesterday afternoon. William Potter, who had care of the room where we work had thrown the belt off the draw, and stopped the brushes where Oxspring was at work. Oxspring had to pull in the wool which the brushes had taken off the shirts and hose. The strap is generally thrown over the seat but it had fallen down. Oxspring reached down behind the back of the seat to get the strap up. I was at the bench near him when the belt caught hold of him by the arm and got wrapped in the shaft and drew him down between the back of the seat and the wall; he was taken round the shaft. I saw his head strike some castings on the floor. When we saw him taken on the shaft, we began shrieking and ran out, there were three boys in the room besides him. Potter came and the engine stopped; I did not see Oxspring taken off the shaft. He was eleven years of age. The deceased was very much injured there were two wounds on the left side of his head and one on his eyebrow; he was not quite dead but only lived a few minutes. Verdict: Accidental death.*'[93]

Accident in a factory through disobeying the safety rules '*An inquest was held on Wednesday 2nd April 1834, at the Queen's Head, Basford, relative to the death of Robert Frost, a single man, aged 32 years. He was employed by Joseph Pearson, bleacher, and engaged as a "getter-up" and whose job was to empty the stockings of the fallers. About seven o'clock that morning he stepped over the shaft which turns the machinery to take up a faller, and as he was returning back over the shaft, he put his foot too far and it was caught by some iron plates. He was then drawn down and his legs, arm and belly, dragged between the shaft and the stone work, which was only four inches apart. Before the engine could be stopped it had torn away the flesh of his belly and drawn out part of his bowels amongst the machinery. It appeared that the workmen had been prohibited from stepping over the shaft but they were in the habit of doing so to save the trouble of going round. He died instantly. Verdict: Accidental death.*'[94]

Fatal accident from piped gas '*An inquest was held on Wednesday 22nd November 1854 at the William IV, Carrington, on the body of John Marriott, labourer, aged 33 years. A sub-contractor who was engaged in laying down gas piping from Nottingham to Basford employed him. On Tuesday afternoon he was instructed to examine a pipe from which gas was escaping near Sherwood Rise. He had uncovered the main pipe that was the source of the leak but in stooping down to his work he had accidentally become suffocated by the noxious fumes. He was discovered lying in a lifeless condition in the hole. He was taken to the William IV public house where every effort was made to restore animation but without success. Verdict: Accidentally suffocated.*'[95]

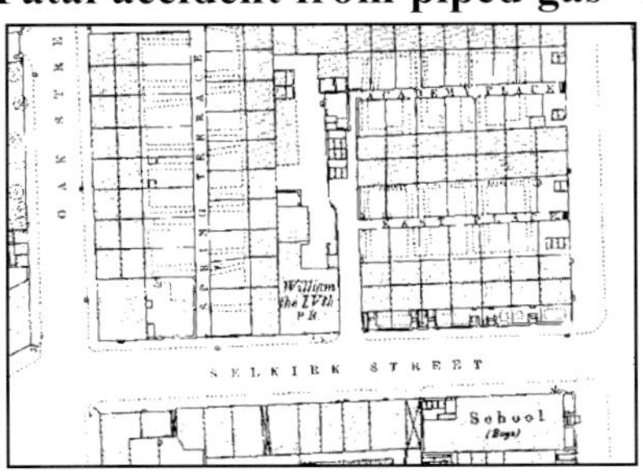

Site of the William IV, Carrington (1882)

Death of a child from falling into a pitch pit '*An inquest was held on Friday 22nd December 1865 at the Waggon & Coals, Mansfield, on the body of Robert Moult aged four years. His father worked at the gas works and his son had gone there one morning to fetch his breakfast tin. In order to reach his father, Robert had attempted to walk across a lake of pitch but*

Waggon & Coals, Mansfield (1970)

although it was glazed over it had not set. It could not bear his weight and he was burnt on his left hand, his legs and knees where the pitch stuck to him. It had been heated to a temperature of 240 to 250 degrees. Medical assistance was obtained but he died a few days later. Apparently he had crossed the pitch on many previous occasions but it was then quite cold. It was understood other boys who went to the yard were in the habit of sliding on the pitch. The jury returned a verdict that the deceased was accidentally burnt and recommended that a fence should be placed around the pitch pit to prevent accidents in the future.'[96]

13. Accidental deaths on the railways

Transporting cattle by train (1843)

The growth of the new railway system in the county presented both the workforce and the public with a potential for accidents. During these early years Coroner Swann presided over a number of inquests relating to death on the network. Accidents sometimes happened when railway personnel were in breach of regulations that resulted in fatalities to staff or passengers. On other occasions deaths occurred when members of the public were incautiously crossing the railway at designated points:

A railway guard disregarded the safety rules '*An inquest was held on the 9th May 1840 at the Victoria Hotel, Beeston, on view of the body of John Hind. He had recently been appointed as a guard on the Nottingham to Derby railway line. Yesterday (Friday), when the afternoon train had just passed Beeston he commenced collecting tickets and in doing this (contrary to his instructions) he went from carriage to carriage, on the steps of the moving train, obviously a most dangerous practice. When placing his feet on the buffers at the end of a carriage, to enable him to pass to the other side, he slipped and fell. The wheels of the next carriage ran over him and severed his head; he was very much injured. The train was immediately stopped and he was taken to the Victoria Hotel, a headless trunk. There appeared to be some doubt whether or not the train driver had received a signal from the other guard to start the train at Beeston station before Hind had finished collecting the tickets. Verdict: Accidentally killed.'*[97]

Victoria Hotel, Beeston (1998)

Accident on a railway crossing '*An inquest was held on the 27th November 1850, at the Yew Tree, Hucknall Torkard, on the body of William Hemshall alias Moody, aged 61 years. The train from Nottingham to Mansfield was proceeding on its way, when near Hucknall Torkard, and crossing a footway from that village to Bulwell it unfortunately came into contact with the deceased. The man was a well-known mole-catcher in the district but he was utterly deaf. He appears not to have seen the train approaching and he was struck by one of the buffers and carried for several yards along the line. Verdict: Accidentally killed by being knocked down by a railway train.'*[98]

Fatal railway accident '*An inquest was held on the 23rd June 1866, at the Bull's Head, Mansfield touching the death of an old woman named Julia Hingley, who was killed on the railway line the previous day. She*

Bull's Head, Mansfield (1970)

lived at Bleakhills outside Mansfield and on her way into the town she had to cross the railway at a place called Tenter-lane crossing. In doing so at about 11.30 on that fatal morning she was struck by the engine of a train which was leaving Mansfield for Nottingham. The driver and fireman were unaware of the accident until they reached Nottingham. Her son said that his mother was very deaf but she had good eyesight. Visibility along the line was good in both directions and there had never previously been an accident at this crossing before. The verdict of the jury was that the deceased was accidentally knocked down by a railway engine and killed and they were of the opinion that a gate should be put up at the side of the railway for the safety of the public. The Mansfield station-master and one of the company's inspectors were present at the inquest and promised that the suggestion of the jury should be attended to at once.'[99]

14. Accidental deaths in the home

Many fatal accidents that occurred in the home were the result of falls, usually down the stairs, very young children when they were being carried tended to be especially vulnerable. Quite often the main source of light on a dark winter evening would have been the candle flame and a mother or nursemaid could easily trip or stumble with a child in their arms in the gloom on the stairs. In the poorer houses the upper rooms were reached, not by conventional stairs, but by ladders that were even more hazardous to ascend and descend. Other fatal accidents resulted from falls down the steps leading to a cellar. In a few other incidents people died from falling out of windows:

A young girl fell down a flight of stairs carrying a baby *'An inquest was held on Friday 14th July 1843 at the Ram, Mansfield Woodhouse, on view of the body of Eliza Huntington, aged thirteen months. Jane Marsh being examined, but not sworn, said I go now and then to Mrs. Huntington's to nurse the child (the deceased) and I was there all last Wednesday. In the evening I went upstairs into the chamber with the child and when I came down again, with the child in my arms, my foot slipped and we both fell to the bottom of the nine steps of the stairs. Mrs. Huntington gave me a pair of old shoes last Wednesday but they were too large and they caused me to fall. The child's neck was dislocated. Verdict: Died in consequence of accidentally falling down a flight of stairs.'*[100]

A charwoman fell down the cellar steps *'An inquest was held on Wednesday 28th May 1834 at the Manver's Arms, Radcliffe-on-Trent, on view of the body of Mary Spencer, aged about 50 years. It appears in evidence that the deceased was employed as a charwoman at the house of Richard Butler, in that village. On Tuesday morning about half-past eight o'clock, she mistook the cellar door for the kitchen door (they both being alike and standing close together), and fell to the bottom of the cellar steps. Immediately assistance was rendered but she was totally insensible. By the evidence of Mr. Ward, surgeon, the deceased had been attacked by apoplexy caused by the fall and after lingering until three o'clock in the afternoon she expired. The deceased has left a husband and nine children. It is worthy of note that Mr. Butler's mother, his wife and several other people have fallen down the same steps. Verdict: Accidental death.'*[101]

Manver's Arms, Radcliffe-on-Trent (1998)

15. Accidentally killed by windmill machinery or by a windmill sail

There were many windmills throughout the County of Nottinghamshire and apart from the unguarded machinery therein which was hazardous both to adults and children, the revolving sails on some mills were an especial danger to children. A number of inquests were held on the bodies of youngsters, between the ages of 3 and 9 years who had died as a consequence of being struck on the head by the sail of a windmill:

The miller's son at Sneinton was the victim of a windmill sail accident '*An inquest was held on Sunday 17th March 1839, at the sign of the Fox, Sneinton, on view the body of Joseph Paling. The deceased, aged five years, was the son of George Paling, miller, of Windmill Hill, Sneinton. ... On the previous Saturday, about one o'clock, the deceased and his brother, aged seven years, went into the mill where their father was at work. They stayed at the mill about a quarter of an hour and then went out. In two minutes after their father followed them down the steps with the intention of shutting the round-house door. The mill was going at three parts her speed but as he was going towards the round-house, he saw the deceased lying on the ground. ... His skull was completely smashed-in and a bit of bone was found on the windmill sail, with which no doubt he had been struck as it was turning. His brother did not see the accident. The children had been frequently cautioned about approaching the windmill sails, when going, and had appeared very careful. Verdict: That a windmill sail accidentally killed the deceased.*'[102]

Sneinton Windmill (c.1870)

Another fatal windmill sail accident at a Sneinton mill 'A*n inquest was held on Friday 29th April 1842 at the Fox, Sneinton, to ascertain the cause of the death of Robert Houlton Knight, three years and nine months old. He was the son of William Knight, timber merchant, Sneinton. On the 18th March, the child went to play in Mr. Bennett's mill yard and unfortunately was struck by one of the sails while the mill was at work. The injury to his head, though every attention was paid by Mr. Hawksley, surgeon, caused his death on Friday morning 29th April 1842 at half past seven o'clock. Verdict: Died in consequence of his skull being accidentally fractured by a windmill sail, the property of John Bennett, of Nottingham, miller and baker. The jury being of the opinion that the gate into the mill yard is not sufficient protection against accidents and strongly recommend Mr. Bennett to have it made more secure.*'[103]

Fox, Sneinton (1977)

Young man killed while oiling the machinery at Keyworth windmill '*An inquest was held on the 1st July 1835 at the Salutation, Keyworth, relative to the death of John Allsop, aged 18 years. It appears that on the previous day, while the rest of the family were in the hay field, he was attending to the windmill. Unfortunately while he was oiling the mechanism he slipped and he became entangled in the cog-wheels crushing his neck, face and his right hand. He languished until the evening when he died from the injuries so received. Verdict: Accidental death with a deodand of 6d. on the machinery.*'[104]

Salutation, Keyworth (1998)

16. Accidentally died in a well

The numerous wells in Nottinghamshire were a potential hazard particularly to children. There are many reports of fatal accidents arising from children falling into uncovered or otherwise unprotected wells. A number of adult deaths also occurred during the sinking of wells or at the time of their repair:

A child falls down a well at Beeston *'An inquest was held on Wednesday 25th June 1834 at the White Lion, Beeston, relative to the death of James Wright, aged two years. It appears that on Monday afternoon, his mother had taken him to the Infant School but at some point he strayed into the yard of the National School and fell into the well. After a short time he was discovered and Joseph Lowe, a pot hawker, descended the well, being twenty feet deep, and brought the child out alive. Unfortunately he died the next day from bruises received in the fall and from inflammation of the lungs. Verdict: Accordingly.'*[105]

A child falls down a well at Sutton-in-Ashfield *'An inquest was held on Tuesday 28th August 1838 at the Bell Inn, Sutton-in-Ashfield, relative to the death of Samuel Parker, aged five years. On last Saturday he went to the well for the purpose of drinking out of the water bucket; while standing on the cover of the well it tipped up and he fell in. A child four years old gave the alarm but it took half an hour to get the deceased out of the well. Verdict: Accidental death.'*[106]

Bell Inn, Sutton-in-Ashfield (1998)

An accident when sinking a well at Radford *'An inquest was held on Saturday 22nd October 1842 at the White Cow beerhouse, Radford, touching the death of Thomas Lowe, aged 77 years. On Monday the 17th instant, he and his son were employed ... to sink a well. When they got down ten feet they erected fan poles over the mouth of the well but the pin that held the poles together came out and the poles fell on to the head of the deceased. He was carried home and attended by Dr. Lightfoot, surgeon, but he died from inflammation of the lungs brought about by the accident. Verdict: Died in consequence of being accidentally hit by the falling of certain fan poles upon him.'*[107]

An accident when sinking a well at East Leake *'An inquest was held on Friday 14th October 1831 at the Three Horse Shoes, East Leake, on view of the body of William Porter. He was employed in sinking a well and had been cautioned not to descend without first letting a candle down because the "damp" had been very bad. ... The man however descended to a depth of 31 yards but he soon perceived that the foul air was too powerful for him and called to be drawn up. When he was about half way up his hands left hold of the rope and he fell overpowered by the mephitic gas that arose. Thirty minutes later his body was recovered and it was discovered that his skull had been fractured by the fall. Verdict: Accidental death.'*[108]

Three Horse Shoes, East Leake (1931)

17. Accidental deaths of children at play

There were a number of inquests on the bodies of children who had received accidental injuries whilst out playing, from which they subsequently died. These varied from unfortunate accidents which occurred whilst taking part in the usual childrens' games or when playing in areas where there was obviously a degree of risk:

Admiral Rodney, Calverton (1925)

An accident while playing at a game called skinny *'An inquest was held on the 3rd January 1835 at the Admiral Rodney, Calverton, on view of the body of William Baines aged eight years. The deceased was playing at skinny, with another boy, named Fletcher and the latter in the act of striking the nogg off, accidentally let his skinny come out of his hand and it hit the deceased on the eye. He was taken home immediately and the surgeon from Arnold saw him on the following Saturday, when the upper eyelid was very much swelled and turgid and the white of the eye very oedematous. On Wednesday evening symptoms of lockjaw were apparent and he died on the following day. Verdict: Accidental death.'*[109]

Young boy falls from a train *'An inquest was held on the 3rd June 1835 at the Bull & Butcher, Selston, relative to the death of John Wharnby, aged five years. It appears that on the evening of the previous Thursday the deceased and another lad had got on to the last waggon in a train of ten waggons loaded with coal. He unfortunately slipped off and his legs were caught between the wheel and the body of the waggon. The flesh of his right leg was torn from the knee to the ankle. Mr. Valentine, surgeon, attended and dressed the wound, but the nervous system had received such a shock as to cause his death on Saturday. The boys had no business on the gang road and the driver had desired them not to get on the waggons. Verdict: Accidental death.'*[110]

Bull & Butcher, Selston (2001)

18. Accidental deaths associated with exposure to cold weather

Sometimes juries considered that the death of a child and sometimes that of an adult, was associated directly or indirectly with the exposure to inclement weather:

A recently-born baby is exposed to cold weather *'An inquest was held on the 1st April 1845, at the Horse & Groom, Moorgreen, on the body of William Henshaw Leavers, aged three weeks. On Sunday last his mother took the infant with her to Bagthorpe and from her evidence she said that the child suffocated because of her anxiety to protect him from the weather. The jury however returned a verdict: That the child died from convulsions by being exposed to the cold weather, he being of a too tender age to endure it.'*[111]

Exposed to cold weather when sleeping out-of-doors *'An inquest was held on the 9th March 1841, at the Rein Deer, East Bridgford, on view the body of William Sharpe, aged 38 years. On Sunday night he went to bed, having a troublesome cough, the following morning he was found quite dead. Mr. Wright, surgeon, was sent for and gave his opinion that he had died from inflammation of the lungs. The deceased was considered a drinking man and would spend all his earnings on drink; he frequently slept in barns and under hay stacks and has done so during this severe winter. Verdict: Found dead in bed and the jury believe he* *died of natural causes (to wit) inflammation of the lungs, caused by excessive drinking and being exposed to the cold in sleeping out at night.'*[112]

19. Struck by lightning

There were a few instances in which farm workers were killed by being struck by lightning whilst sheltering in the fields, during a thunderstorm:

Accident in Ruddington *'An inquest was held on the 19th July 1828 at the Red Heart, Ruddington, on view of the body of John Hemsley, aged 23 years. The deceased was a servant of Mr. Cripwell's, maltster, Ruddington and was working on a farm the previous morning and the horse and cart returned without him. It was found that he had taken shelter under a tree and had been struck by lightning. His lips were swollen and black and his face was also discoloured. He was quite dead when found. Verdict: Accidental death by lightning.'*[113]

Red Heart, Ruddington (1929)

Accident in Radcliffe-on-Trent *'An inquest was held on the 27th March 1846, at the Manver's Arms, Radcliffe-on-Trent, upon the bodies of two farm labourers, William Scothern and John Caunt. They were working in a field, when a violent storm broke out. Later a boy was sent into a nearby field to fetch in some cows but when he returned he said that one of them had died after having been struck by lightning. At that time he did not see the deceased at work but he noticed that the door of a hovel was open and he supposed that they were taking shelter. At nine o'clock however, as they had not returned to their homes, their employer and two servants went in search of them with a lantern. On arriving at the hovel they were found, both in sitting positions; both were dead. They were locked in the hovel overnight and removed the following morning. Scothern at the time of the awful visitation had on a pair of new boots the soles of which were covered in bright nails. Three of these nails were knocked out and it was thought that the electric fluid had passed out through his feet. There was also a small hole in the boot of Caunt and his shirt and other garments were torn on his left side. The hair of both their heads was much singed and their flannel waistcoats were considerably scorched. It is evident that they died without a struggle. Verdict: That the two deceased were struck by electric fluid in a thunderstorm and killed.'*[114]

20. Disease – cholera etc.

Many persons during this period died from infectious or contagious diseases, these included scarlet fever, typhus, typhoid and cholera. It was rare for them to be brought to the attention of the coroner because the reasons for death would be very apparent to the medical profession. The coroner and his jury would also be less than enthusiastic to attend an inquest where there was little doubt that a transmittable disease was the cause of death. Nevertheless there were a number of occasions where they were asked to investigate a death, that was possibly suspicious, but later confirmed to be the result of natural disease:

Manver's Arms, Radcliffe-on-Trent (1998)

Cholera at Radcliffe-on-Trent *'An inquest was held on the 26th September 1849, at the Manver's Arms, Radcliffe-on-Trent, on the body of Jane Caunt, aged three years. Sarah Bell said that she was called in to nurse the deceased child's* *mother who was ill with Asiatic cholera. Yesterday morning the child also became ill, being very sick and purged and turned dark-coloured, we fomented the child's bowels with hot flannels and also her legs and feet because she had violent cramps. Mr. Martin, the surgeon, came and ordered some medicine but she would not take it. She was in a state of complete collapse, her hands and feet were drawn up and she was insensible. The vomiting and purging continued until four o'clock in the afternoon when the child died. I have seen several cases of cholera having been a nurse in Nottingham some years ago, when the disease prevailed and I have not the slightest doubt the child died of that disease. Her grandmother was taken ill of cholera yesterday morning and died in the evening. I expect the child's mother to die of cholera very soon. There is a privy under one of the bedrooms and it projects into the house creating a very bad smell. There is a sough against the house door, which throws out a noxious stench. There are many other privies in the neighbourhood and a pigsty above the house, which smells very disagreeable. A number of other persons in the same street have died or are dying of cholera. The street goes by the name of Mount Pleasant! I have never heard of any Sanitary Board being established in this village nor have I seen any person inspecting the place for nuisances. I have not seen or known of any means being used to clean out the sewers, to whitewash the houses or improve the state of the village. The parents of the deceased child have taken in lodgers who were generally navvies, as many as five or six at a time. There are seven persons of their own family living in the house beside the lodgers, which consists of only four small rooms. William Martin who attended the deceased child, described the symptoms, and had no doubt she died of Asiatic cholera of a very malignant form. He considered the neighbourhood to be in a very unhealthy and over-crowded state. The cholera broke out there about three weeks ago and there have been 11 cases since then, six of them fatal. Diarrhoea prevailed to a considerable extent. Verdict: Death from Asiatic cholera.*'[115]

Cholera at Basford '*An inquest was held on the 17th November 1849 at the Shoulder of Mutton, Basford, upon the body of James Brown, aged 68 years. He had enjoyed good health until recently. On Friday morning he complained to his son that during the night he had had violent purging and sickness. He became worse and Mr. Morley, surgeon, came to see him, he was very troubled with cramp which caused large lumps on his legs, but as fast as they were rubbed down they came up in another place. Every attention was paid to him but he died early on Saturday morning. Others in the family had or were still ill with diarrhoea. Their neighbours were also ill with cholera. The area is in a most filthy state and the air is poisoned by manure-heaps, ash-pits, pigsties and privies all open to the atmosphere. Verdict: Death from Asiatic cholera.*'[116]

Typhus Fever at Sherwood '*An inquest was held on Sunday 26th November 1837 at Mr. William Clower's the sign of the "Hit or Miss, Luck's All," Sherwood in the Parish of Basford, on the body of a stranger who had given his name as Thomas Adison. It appeared that in the morning of Wednesday 15th instant, the deceased crossed over the Mansfield Road as if he came out of Basford Lane and went into the cow hovel adjoining Mr. Clower's house. He staggered as he crossed the road; Mrs. Clower together with the person who saw him enter the hovel found him lying on his side with his head resting on a piece of wood under the manger. Mr. Clower came and he was taken upstairs and placed near a fire ...He was stiff and cold and complained of pains in his head, stomach and side. Shortly after he was discovered in the hovel the Parish Officer was informed and he received medical assistance, he was bled and given medicine, which gave him temporary relief. However, two days later he was attacked by typhus fever and he became delirious and died on Sunday the 19th November. Verdict: Death in consequence of typhus fever.*'[117]

The venue of this inquest, which went by the strange name of the "Hit or Miss, Luck's All", was almost certainly one of the beer houses that were allowed to operate, by Act of Parliament (11 Geo. IV & 1.Wm. 1 c. 64.), between the 10th October 1830 and 15th

July 1869 (32 & 33 Vict. c. 27.). It was open to all householders assessed to the poor rate to apply for an excise licence that was renewable annually on payment of a fee of two pounds two shillings to sell beer, ale or porter from their premises. They were obliged to erect a board outside their house on which the name of the person holding the licence was to be displayed in letters three inches in length Many would also give their outlet a distinguishing name but it was not obligatory and it seems very likely that the names may have been frequently altered, particularly on change of ownership. Unfortunately these excise records or those held by the magistrates or police authorities do not appear to have survived within Nottinghamshire. The description given in the above inquest places the beer house on Mansfield Road opposite to Basford Lane (now known as Haydn Road) and would have been on the site of, or became in the early 1860's, the Robin Hood public house.

21. Still-born

It was not uncommon to find newly-born children abandoned soon after birth and at subsequent inquests the question was raised whether the child actually breathed after birth. A still-born child is not a person within the meaning of a Coroner's Act and it was assumed that every child '*is presumed to have been born dead*' until the contrary was proved.[1] Live birth can only be proved by medical testimony after a post-mortem examination. A coroner has jurisdiction only in cases where a person has died and therefore an anomalous situation arises. However, where it could be shown that the child had not breathed then it was the custom to record a verdict of '*found dead or still-birth.*' If the medical evidence demonstrated that the child had breathed then the verdict would be recorded as '*wilful murder usually by a person or persons unknown*':

A suspicious burial in Gedling '*An inquest was held on the 28th February 1850, at the Chesterfield Arms, Gedling on the body of a newly-born male infant, which had been buried in the churchyard under suspicious circumstances. It appears that about six o'clock on the evening previous to the present inquisition, Joseph Hemstock, constable, learnt that a newly-born infant had been found buried in Gedling churchyard and on proceeding to the place discovered an old tea chest lying upon the mound of a grave. The box contained a dead child wrapped up in some hay and a napkin. On the following day a post-mortem examination was made on the body by Mr. Sanford Tatham Davison, surgeon, and from the appearances he observed, he had no doubt the deceased was still-born and the jury returned a verdict to this effect.*'[118]

Chesterfield Arms, Gedling (1998)

The body of a child is secretly buried '*An inquest was held on the 18th and by adjournment on Friday 21st April 1854, at the Royal Oak, Oxton, on the body of a male child, the illegitimate son of Mary Robinson, single woman, now deceased. Miss Robinson was housekeeper to her brother, George Robinson, farmer, of Greaves near Oxton and was 26 years of age. Her family never for a moment suspected the circumstance of her being enceinte. However, shortly before noon on Sunday 2nd April she gave birth to a child the subject of the present enquiry. No one was with her in the room at the time and the birth was alleged to be premature and the child still-born. George Robinson, observing that his sister looked very ill fetched her aunt to look after her and to this person Miss Robinson related all that had occurred. On Monday, Mr. Calvert of Southwell, surgeon, was called in, he found*

Miss Robinson in a dreadful state of exhaustion, consequent upon want of proper attention, from the effects of which she died on Thursday the 13th. Her aunt, anxious to gratify her niece's desire of secrecy had the child privately buried in Edingley churchyard but by the direction of the coroner, it was after the lapse of one week disinterred. Mr. Calvert made a critical examination of the body and confirmed that the child had been still-born and the jury returned a verdict to this effect. At the same time they expressed their extreme disgust at the manner in which the aunt of Miss Robinson had disposed of the body of the child, previous to its legal burial.'[119]

A headless child's body found in a load of manure '*An inquest was held on the 7th April 1843 at William Wilde's, farmer, Owthorpe, on a certain female child. Thomas Lockton, of Kinoulton, on being examined said he was employed on Friday 31st of March last, in unloading a boat of manure, which had been brought from Nottingham, for Thomas Wilde. While employed in filling the wheelbarrows and wheeling them from the boat to the land, he found a body of a female child in the manure, wrapped up in a rag, with its head off. The boatmen placed the child on top of the manure heap and the witness and the boatmen left Owthorpe in the evening leaving the child on the manure heap. The following day the witness was sent by his master to the manure heap to collect the child but after turning the heap over for some time he could not find it. On Wednesday the witness was taken by a policeman before a magistrate who charged him with concealing the body of a child and he was ordered to go again and try and find it. He returned the next day and after searching for half an hour found it buried in the manure and the body was taken to the Parish Church. Mr. Marriott, surgeon, of Colston Basset, examined the body and found that the head had been separated from the body, not by any sharp instrument but it appeared to him to have been torn off, as the upper part of the chest, the lungs and windpipe were missing. It had every appearance of being eaten off by a cat or vermin; the child was not a full-grown one and he was of the opinion that it was not born alive. Verdict: Still-born.'*[120]

22. Miscarriage

Deaths associated with child-birth were not uncommon but few would be brought to the attention of the coroner. However, when a miscarriage happened an inquest was sometimes called for in order to ascertain that the event was a natural occurrence or to determine whether or not there were any mitigating circumstances associated with the death:

Died from cold and neglect '*An inquest was held on the 22nd July 1847 at the Brown Cow, Mansfield, upon Ann Bramwell, a single woman, aged 25 years. It appears that about a fortnight previous to her death she miscarried, took cold and became very ill but refused to have a doctor. On Monday morning she rapidly became much worse and Mr. Turner, surgeon was sent for; he found her in a dying state and directed small quantities of brandy to be given to her but she never rallied and expired in about four hours. Mr. Turner made a post-mortem examination and ascribed her death to inflammation of the peritoneum, the effects of taking cold and subsequent neglect. Verdict: Accordingly.'*[121]

Brown Cow, Mansfield (c.1908)

23. Intoxication

Deaths directly attributable to or accelerated by excessive drinking frequently featured in the verdicts of inquests. Beer (or ale) was regarded as an important commodity, it was a popular beverage at every meal at a time when water or even milk were not considered pure and all but a small minority of the population enjoyed drinking. However, whilst drunkenness may very well be related to the over-indulgence of beer it was invariably the excess intake of ardent spirits (alcoholic distilled liquors) that led directly to the demise of some individuals or enhanced the effects of concomitant disease. Drunkenness may well however be an indirect cause of accidental death, for instance, falling down the stairs or drowning:

Over-indulgence in drinking ardent spirits *'An inquest was held on the 26th June 1851 at the Sherwood Inn, Sherwood, on the body of Henry Thrall, aged 36. On the 24th June the deceased and two colleagues, William Ball and John Guyler were installing a pump to empty a cesspool at Mrs. Burton's, Woodville House, Sherwood. About two o'clock, Jonathan Burton jun., went to see how they were getting on and invited them to have a glass of beer but Guyler said they would prefer something better. They were provided with brandy but there was also whiskey, rum, gin and sherry in liquor stands on the sideboard. They were left in the room together during which time they had access to what they liked. Mr. Burton returned after about a quarter of an hour when he found they had whiskey, rum and brandy on the table, and the men had glasses before them partly filled with brandy. They wanted more liquor but it was refused, as it was evident that they had already had too much. Thrall eventually became sick, vomited a little and became so helpless that he was unable to speak. Ball carried him into a stable and a surgeon was sent for who applied the usual restoratives but the deceased never rallied and he was carried home but he soon died. The deceased has left a wife and eight children. The jury returned a verdict of death from excessive drinking. Guyler was also taken very ill and died a few days later and an inquest was also held on his body at the Sherwood Inn and an identical verdict reached. Ball who had taken very much less alcohol survived.'*[122]

Three inebriated men

Fell into a brook in a state of intoxication *'An inquest was held on the 26th September 1838, at the Cross Keys, Arnold, touching the death of Gervas German, aged 67 years. On Monday night, it being Arnold feast, he and others were drinking at the above public house and at nine o'clock he rose to go out of the house, when Mrs. Dickinson said, "are you going home?" He answered "no" he was going to come in again. The night was very dark and it was raining very fast. The deceased was very fresh in liquor and when staggering out struck himself against the door. Ten minutes afterwards, he was found in the brook, which runs through the Town Street, with his body excepting one shoulder under the water. He was taken out, carried to the Cross Keys public house and put to bed, a surgeon was sent for and every possible means used to revive him but to no avail and he died later that night. The brook was swollen in consequence of the rain and was about a foot and a half deep; there is no guard, fence or protection whatever to it and there is no doubt but that he accidentally fell in and was unable to help himself. Verdict: Died in consequence of accidentally falling into the Town Street brook, he being in a state of intoxication at the time.'*[123]

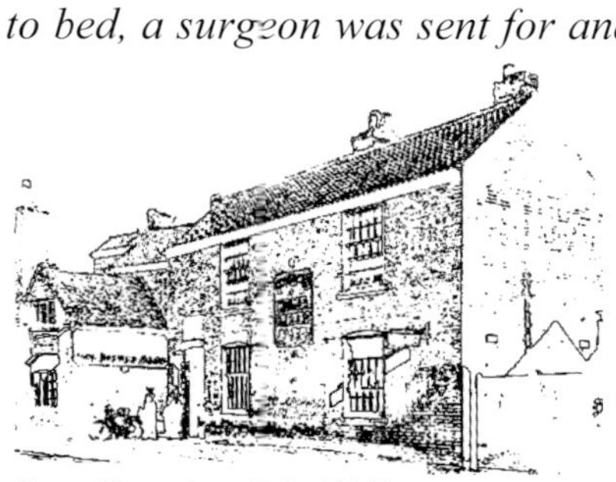

Cross Keys, Arnold (c.1910)

24. Died in a balloon accident

On Monday 24th August 1863 a Grand Fête was held in the grounds of Basford Hall and was attended by thousands of visitors. A feature of the day's merriment was the ascent by a well-known aeronaut in a gas-filled balloon. Unfortunately problems arose in inflating the balloon and the owner, Henry Coxhill, announced that he was too heavy to make the ascent and proposed to make an unmanned flight. However a local man, James Chambers,[124] volunteered to take his place as he was much lighter and indeed had previous experience in ballooning. Coxhill agreed but regrettably this decision was disastrous for the balloon crashed in Arnold and James Chambers was killed. An inquest was held in the evening of the next day and lasted four hours, the proceeding are summarised:

Accident at Basford fête '*An inquest was held on Tuesday 25th August 1863, at the Robin Hood Inn, Arnold, on the body of James Chambers, aged 37 years. Henry Coxhill was examined and said he was the aeronaut who had accepted an engagement to go up in a balloon at a fête to be held in Basford Park. He arrived on Sunday afternoon, his balloon was a new one and he had not previously made an ascent in it. He commenced the process of filling the balloon with gas throughout the night and when it was inflated he tried it three times but found that it was not sufficiently buoyant to carry his weight. At that point James Chambers came along and on hearing of Coxhill's difficulty volunteered to take his place as he was less heavy. It seems that Coxhill had been acquainted with the father of Chambers and he then agreed to his request and he knew that he had ascended in balloons on previous occasions. The ascent was unremarkable but it was on the descent that the disaster happened. An eyewitness said that the balloon was swaying as it descended as if there was an escape of gas. The body of the balloon seemed to cover the car and it landed soon afterwards. When he reached the car the man was nearly dead and there was a pocket-handkerchief placed against his mouth. The car had bounded about two yards, there was a very strong smell of gas, they got him out and laid him on the grass but he died shortly afterwards. Henry Coxhill gave his opinion on the cause of the accident. He said that after Chambers had emerged from the clouds the balloon entered into sunshine which caused the gas to rapidly expand and stream out of the neck or the safety valve, which is always left open. By being found with a handkerchief in his mouth it is evident that he was inhaling the gas which might have been prevented by slightly opening the upper valves. It was supposed that he became insensible from the effects of the gas. The jury returned the following verdict: That the deceased, James Chambers, ascended in the balloon in a voluntary manner of his own free will. Through inhaling the gas he became insensible and incapable of working the balloon properly and that the balloon coming into violent contact with the earth caused his death.*'[125]

Rural and musical fête at Basford Park (1859)

Robin Hood & Little John, Arnold (1998)

James Chambers was buried in the General Cemetery, Nottingham, on Sunday, 30th August 1863; the funeral was attended by a large number of mourners.

During the mid-Victorian era ballooning was becoming a popular pastime amongst certain members of the public. Indeed there were a number of so-called professionals who gave displays at fêtes throughout the country. There had been a number of accidents on previous occasions and the Illustrated London News was forthright in its condemnation of the ascent in a pleasure balloon as being '*a senseless, bootless and perilous exhibition and should be prohibited.*'[126]

25. Suicide

Unfortunately, taking one's life was not an uncommon occurrence and coroners had to preside over many inquests of this nature. To some extent, it is tempting to blame the social conditions of the period, for the majority of suicides were amongst the poorer classes and may well have been precipitated by a feeling of despair, caused by either financial or health worries. Swann maintained that '*the very act of self destruction is evidence of insanity because he could not imagine that any person in the full vigour of his mind would, for instance, put a pistol to his head and blow his brains out. He considered that there must be a diseased mind before a man could bring himself to such a resolution.*' Therefore we see that in the overwhelming number of recorded verdicts that it is stated that the deceased took his or her own life during a period of temporary insanity. Occasionally juries could not always come to a firm decision on this point and so added a rider '*but whether the deceased was of sound or unsound mind at the time no sufficient evidence seems to prove.*' Both these verdicts had very important connotations for it meant that in an age of strong religious fervour the burial of the person could be performed with all the attendant rites. Only on three occasions was a verdict of suicide reached in Swann's court when it was stated that the person was of sound mind. This was called '*felo-de-se*' and then the coroner was obliged to command that the burial was to take place during the night without any of the normal religious rites. None of these burials were entered in the parish registers and as the deaths occurred before the advent of civil registration, the only surviving record is in the pages of the local press. An account of such an event that occurred subsequent to the implementation of the Births & Deaths Registration Act of 1836 (6 & 7 Will IV c.86) has been noted in a parish outside Nottinghamshire:

'*About nine o'clock on Friday night, a common cart drawn by an old horse emerged from the hospital gates. The end of a deal coffin hung over the tailboard and the name Williams written on it with a bit of chalk. The night watchman at the cemetery was called and informed of the business in hand. A messenger was sent to the neighbouring public house and was fortunate enough to find two gravediggers there. These men were promptly set to work and dug a grave. The coffin was lowered into its place and the earth was instantly shovelled down and stamped in, the torchlight extinguished and all was over.*'[127]

It was not until 1882, long after Swann's death, that the power of a coroner to direct the interment of the remains of persons found '*felo-de-se*' was abolished by an Act of Parliament (45 & 46 Vict. c.19).

Persons took their own lives by hanging or shooting themselves, cutting their throats, taking poison (usually arsenic), drowning, or jumping out of windows:

Woodborough – suicide of a young married woman by hanging '*An inquest was held on Saturday 25th September 1847 at the Cock & Falcon, Woodborough, upon Elizabeth Hogg wife of John Hogg, farmer, Woodborough. Sarah Richardson, aged 15, deposed that she was a servant to the deceased. On the morning of the day prior to the inquest, Elizabeth Hogg brought her six-month old baby to her and asked her to wash and dress it as she was feeling sick and was going to lie down. ... When Mr. Hogg came in from his farm for his dinner at twelve o'clock, he was told that his wife was upstairs. ... He went to search for her and found her in the garret, she was hanging by a noose and was quite cold and dead. He fetched Mr. Osbourne, surgeon, and together they cut her down. It seems that for some time past she had suffered from pains in her head, which greatly troubled her. The jury returned a verdict of: Hung herself during a temporary state of insanity.*'[128]

Suicide by hanging at Wollaton Hall '*An inquest was held on Monday 15th January 1849 at the King's Head, Wollaton, on the body of Thomas Jordan, aged 52 years. He was employed in sweeping the chimneys of Wollaton Hall, the seat of Lord Middleton and was assisting Simon Hancock, a chimney sweep of Radford. They had swept all the chimneys except one that could only be done by going to the top of the Hall and descending the chimney. As Hancock was ascending the steps of the north turret to look for the deceased he found him hanging by a rope and quite dead. He called for assistance and the body was cut down and put in a cart and taken home. ... A witness said he had thought, for some time, that the deceased was not right in his mind and that he had on previous occasions, attempted to destroy himself. Verdict: Hung himself during a temporary fit of insanity.*'[129]

Wollaton Hall (1821)

Suicide of a Sneinton clergyman by shooting himself '*An inquest was held on Saturday evening 11th November 1848 at the Gate public house, Brewhouse Yard, Nottingham on the body of the Reverend William Brown, a curate of the Church of England in Sneinton. He was 25 years old. Apparently he had become affectionately inclined to a young lady, aged 17 years, the daughter of another clergyman, the Reverend Edward Bull, incumbent of St. James's in Nottingham. On making his feelings known to her father, the latter in consideration of her youth, kindly advised William Brown to endeavour to put out of his mind, at any rate for the time being, any expectations he had towards his daughter. On the day he received the letter to this effect Brown became very agitated and left his lodgings in a hurry and went to John Jackson, gunsmith, in Church Gate, Nottingham, and purchased a pistol, a flask of powder, shot and caps costing 28s. He then it appears went up to the Nottingham Castle Yard and shot himself. His body was discovered during the evening of Friday 10th November and in his waistcoat pocket was the letter from Edward Bull. The jury returned a verdict of temporary insanity.*'[130]

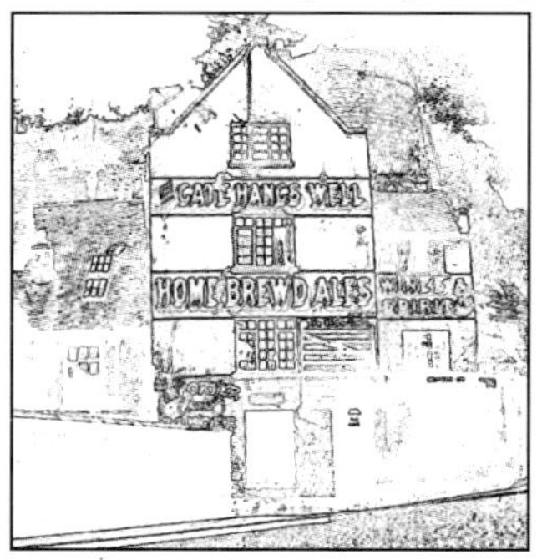

Gate Hangs Well, Brewhouse Yard (1906)

Suicide of a publican by cutting his throat at Gunthorpe '*An inquest was opened on Tuesday 2nd April 1861 at the Boat* [probably an error should be Anchor] *Inn, to inquire into the death of James Tomlinson, publican* [Anchor], *aged 45 years. It appears from the evidence of Jane Tomlinson, the widow of the deceased, that he got up on Sunday morning about five o'clock. ... About half past six o'clock she heard her son, Frederick, screaming and he told her that his father had committed suicide in the stable adjoining the house. He had cut his throat with a hay-cutting knife. He had been in a low state of mind for some time but* *his wife was not apprehensive that he would commit suicide. Verdict: That the deceased cut his throat in a temporary fit of insanity.'*[131]

Pregnant servant dies from arsenic poisoning *'An inquest was opened at Widmerpool on Thursday 26th April 1838 and then adjourned to the following day at the Boot Inn, Wysall, to inquire into the death of Ann Frisby, aged 19 years. She was a lived-in servant to Joseph Payne, farmer in Widmerpool. It appears from the evidence of two surgeons after a post-mortem examination that she was enceinte one month and died from taking arsenic. A great number of witnesses were examined before the coroner. It appeared that the arsenic had been procured for, or administered by, the son of a respectable person, or at least he was privy to her having taken it but the evidence it seems was inconclusive. The jury after a protracted and patient inquiry returned a verdict: Died as a consequence of taking a dose of arsenic whilst labouring under a temporary fit of insanity.'*[132]

Suicide by drowning at Lenton *'An inquest was held on Monday 21st August 1837 at the White Hart, Lenton, touching the death of Ann Eaton, aged 19 years. On the previous Saturday evening she was found drowned in the local canal by two persons walking along the hauling path. She was a servant with Mrs. Newball of Radford and it appears, in the last few weeks, she had been in a despondent mood on account of a supposed disappointment in a love affair. Verdict: Drowned herself whilst labouring under a fit of temporary insanity.'*[133]

White Hart, Lenton (1930)

Suicide of the station-master at Lowdham *'An inquest was held on the 9th May 1861 at the Railway Public House, Lowdham, on the body of Leonard Moore. On Wednesday morning he left home informing his wife that he was going for a walk but when he did not return for his breakfast she became alarmed. He was later found by the local police constable hanging by his neck in a hovel close to his house. Apparently contrary to his official instructions he had given credit for some goods and feared that he would not be reimbursed before he had to declare his monthly accounts. This appeared to be the cause of his distressed state of mind and he left a note naming the persons who owed him money. Verdict: That the deceased hanged himself during a fit of temporary insanity.'*[134]

Railway Inn, Lowdham (1998)

Suicide (felo-de-se) by hanging and the body buried at night without a service *'An inquest was held on Friday 14th February 1833, at the Swan* [renamed the Lord Nelson in 1841], *Burton Joyce, on view of the body of Hannah Spyby, aged 23 years. The deceased had been a servant to Mr. Clarke for nearly three years. About five years ago she had a child by a man called Iliffe, residing at Lambley, but she used to complain that she had not enough money for its support. Her manners were generally lively and she expressed a strong attachment for Iliffe. For the past week she appeared more thoughtful and got up as usual on Wednesday morning. Mr. Clarke's daughter heard a chair fall and went down the stairs and found the deceased hanging by the neck in the kitchen. She immediately called her father who cut her down but life was extinct. Mr. Billings, surgeon, examined her and ascertained that she was six months advanced in pregnancy. The jury returned a verdict of felo-de-se and the body of the deceased was to be buried, the same night, between the hours of nine and twelve, of course without the usual service of the interment of the dead.'*[135]

26. Murder

Christopher Swann held 44 inquests where the verdict of the jury was that the deceased died as a result of wilful murder. In two of these inquests more than one person was murdered and these eventually became some of the more sensational cases. It is not the purpose of this book to dwell in any great detail on the outcome of any trial of the perpetrator of the crime, who so often became notorious whilst the victim tended to be forgotten:

The verdicts may be divided into two categories:

a. Those where the perpetrator of the crime of murder had not been apprehended.
b. Those where the person had been identified.

In this latter instance the coroner would issue a warrant which would compel the person to appear at the next Assize Court to answer the charge. A list of the latter cases is given in Table 8. It will be noted that of the 23 inquest verdicts of murder only 19 resulted in a trial, three persons took their own lives shortly after the crime and one other person absconded after the inquest. Only in five cases was the verdict of murder in the coroner's court substantiated when the case came to trial and in four others the charge was reduced to manslaughter and one to criminal homicide. In the other instances, the charge was reduced to concealing a birth of a child, or not guilty but insane or not guilty and discharged:

(a) The perpetrator was unknown

(i) Murder by strangulation of a new-born child in Nottingham

'A*n inquest was held at the Trip to Jerusalem, in the extra-parochial district of Brewhouse Yard, Nottingham, on Monday 16th September 1839, on the body of an unknown new-born female child. The body had been discovered in the river Leen when a grating was being cleared, it was taken to the inn where the inquest was later to be held. It was wrapped up in a brown drugget and when opened it was apparent that a cord was tied around its neck. An autopsy was carried out and by the state of the lungs it was clear that the baby had been born alive and further medical examination determined that death was due to strangulation. Although the inquiry had been adjourned for a week no evidence of the identity of the mother was forthcoming. The jury therefore returned a verdict of: Wilful murder by strangulation by some person or persons unknown.*'[136]

Trip to Jerusalem, Brewhouse Yard (1944)

(ii) Murder by strangulation of a new-born child in Bulwell

'*An inquest was held at the Horse & Jockey, Bulwell, by adjournment on Monday 20th December 1847 on view of the body of a new-born female child. She was found in a remote place in Bulwell Spring; she was naked with a piece of tape tied around her neck. An autopsy established that death was caused by strangulation prior to being thrown into the water. A girl, Mary Gent, was suspected of being the mother but her sister categorically denied, on oath, that she had been pregnant. This was supported by a medical opinion. Verdict: Wilful murder by some person or persons unknown.*'[137]

Horse & Jockey, Bulwell (1951)

Table 8.

Inquests of Christopher Swann where the verdict was wilful murder

Place	Venue	Inquest date(s)	Deceased	Age *	Perpetrator (s)
Sutton-in-Ashfield	Black Bull	08.09.1830	George Shooter	53	Henry Shooter [1]
Normanton-on-Soar	house of John Buckley	07.12.1830	unnamed child	<1d.	Maria Warrington [2]
Mansfield	Black Bull	10.10.1833	Hannah Holland	4	Mary Holland [3]
Carrington	William the Fourth	11.10.1836	William Renshaw	n. r.	William Terry [4]
Basford	Fox & Crown	05.04.1837	John Greensmith Wm. Greensmith Ann Greensmith Mark Greensmith	9 7 5 2	Thomas Greensmith [5]
Mansfield	Ram, then adjourned to the Town Hall	01.01.1842	Mary Hallam	19	John Jones [6]
Radford	Pheasant	14,17,02,03.03 1842	Thomas Robinson	70	Benjamin Hurd [7] Hannah Hurd [7]
Colwick & Nottingham	house of Wm. Parr, constable, adjourned to the County Hall	24,27,28.05.1844	Ann Saville Harriet Saville Mary Saville Thomas Saville	38 7 5 3	William Saville [8]
Sutton-in-Ashfield	Devonshire Arms	23,28.01.1850	Mary Hallam	2	George Berry [9]
Radford	Peacock	26.11.1850	Eliza Chambers	3	Charlotte Chambers [10]
Eastwood	Sun	24,27.03.1851 11,16,17.04.1851	Joseph Barber	35	Sarah Barber [11] Robert Ingram [11]
Lenton	Travellers Rest	03.05.1852	Thomas Clarke Lewis	3w.	Emma Lewis [12]
Bingham	Union Workhouse	04,07.12.1852	unnamed child	10d.	Mary Ann Parr [13]
Basford	Horse & Jockey	07,09,10.10.1854	Hemley Pearson	25	Thomas Charlesworth [14]
Beeston	Commercial Inn	04.02.1856	George Burton	56	George Burton the younger [15]
West Leake	Basket	01,02.08.1856	William Gent	6m.	Hannah Gent [16]
Radford	Rose & Crown	18.05.1857	unnamed child	<1d.	Emma Cooke [17]
Annesley	Annesley Hall adjourned to Blue Bell	06.01.1858 12.01.1858	George Wingfield	19	John Draper & others unknown to the jury [18]
Keyworth	Salutation	31.04.1858	Harriet Lacey	6m.	Ann Lacey [19]
Lenton	Grove Tavern	27,30.12.1859 03.01.1860	George Clarke	30	Herbert Slack [20] Alfred Slack [20]
Cossall	no record	27.02.1862	unnamed child	<1d.	Lavinia Martin [21]
Radford	Jolly Higglers	20,24,31.07.1863	unnamed child	<1d.	Rosanna Knight [22]
Carlton	Volunteer	19,23,27,29.11. 1866 13.12.1866 01.01.1867	Henry Raynor	31	John Watson [23] Mary Watson [23]

* n.r. = no record. d. = days w. = weeks m. = months other ages are given in years < = less than

Notes or verdicts reached at subsequent trials

[1] Henry Shooter being of unsound mind stabbed his father, George Shooter, to death and then killed himself with the knife [report on page 70].

[2] Maria Warrington was not charged with the murder of her new-born child but found guilty of concealing the birth and sent to prison for 18 months.

[3] Mary Holland was found not guilty of murdering her child, Hannah Holland, with laudanum but declared insane and that she should remain in prison at Her Majesty's pleasure.

[4] William Terry stabbed William Renshaw but absconded before his trial and a reward of £20 was offered for his apprehension.

[5] Thomas Greensmith was found guilty of the wilful murder of his four children, John, William, Ann and Mark by strangulation and sentenced to be hung; later reprieved and transported for life to New South Wales [report on page 60].

[6] John Jones was found guilty of the wilful murder of Mary Hallam, by stabbing, and sentenced to death and hung in Nottingham on 23rd March 1842 [report on page 67].

[7] Benjamin and Hannah Hurd were accused of adding laudanum to Thomas Robinson's ale at a house in Nottingham with the sole purpose of robbing him. Robinson was later taken home to Radford in a drugged condition from which he never fully recovered and he eventually died. At their trial Benjamin Hurd was acquitted but his wife was found guilty of manslaughter and sentenced to transportation for life and sent to Van Dieman's Land (Tasmania) [report on page 69].

Table 8. (cont.)

Notes or verdicts reached at subsequent trials

8 William Saville was convicted of murdering his wife, Ann, by cutting her throat, he also murdered his three children, Harriet, Mary and Thomas. He was sentenced to death and hung on 7th August 1844 in Nottingham [report on page 62].

9 George Berry was found not guilty of murder by attacking Mary Hallam with a cleaver but judged to be insane and kept in custody until Her Majesty's pleasure was known.

10 Charlotte Chambers being of unsound mind strangulated her daughter and then cut her own throat.

11 Sarah Barber was found guilty of poisoning her husband, Joseph Barber, with arsenic for which she was sentenced to death, but later reprieved and transported for life to Van Dieman's Land (Tasmania). Robert Ingram was declared not guilty and released [report on page 64].

12 Emma Lewis was alleged to have deliberately drowned her child, Thomas Clarke Lewis, in the Nottingham canal. At her trial she was cleared of his murder on the grounds that she was insane at the time.

13 Mary Ann Parr was found guilty of suffocating her child and sentenced to be hung; but this was later commuted to transportation; however she was eventually sent to Broadmoor being of unsound mind [report on page 80].

14 Thomas Charlesworth was found guilty of the manslaughter of Hemley Pearson; whom he had discovered was having an adulterous relationship with his wife. He was sentenced to penal servitude for six years.

15 George Burton the younger was accused of burning coke in the room with little ventilation and so suffocated his father, George Burton, but at his trial he was found not guilty.

16 Hannah Gent murdered her son, William Gent, by poisoning him with arsenic and then hung herself.

17 The charge that Emma Cooke murdered her new-born child was rejected and she was discharged.

18 John Draper was found guilty of manslaughter for shooting George Wingfield and sentenced to seven years penal servitude. His compatriot poachers, were arrested after the coroner's inquest, William Atkinson, Frank Hardy, William Tomlinson, James Beardall, Joseph Burton and John Gelsthorpe acting in cohort with Draper were imprisoned for 18 months.

19 Ann Lacey was acquitted of murdering her daughter, Harriet Lacey by cutting her throat but because of her mental state she was detained at Her Majesty's pleasure.

20 Herbert Slack was found guilty of criminal homicide by stabbing George Clarke and sentenced to penal servitude for 15 years; his brother Alfred was acquitted.

21 Lavinia Martin was found guilty of drowning her child and imprisoned for 10 years for manslaughter.

22 Rosanna Knight was found not guilty of murder but sentenced to three months in prison for concealing the birth of her new-born daughter.

23 This was a case of the suspected murder of Henry Raynor but the coroner Christopher Swann, died before the inquest was concluded and for technical and legal reasons the replacement coroner could not allow the jury to arrive at a verdict and the inquest was terminated. The Watson's were however brought to trial but were acquitted [report on page 85].

(b) The perpetrator was known and sent for trial at the Nottingham Assizes

(i) John, William, Ann and Mark murdered by their father, Thomas Greensmith
[Table 8. footnote 5]

The murder of John, aged nine years, William, aged eight years, Ann, aged five years and Mark Greensmith, three years old, was the subject of an inquest that took place on Wednesday the 5th April 1837 at the Fox & Crown in Basford. It appeared that their father Thomas Greensmith, aged 35 years, had strangled them while they were in bed. Greensmith's wife had died a short time ago and he lived with a housekeeper in a small house behind the Fox & Crown public house and it was in an upper room of this building that the murder took place and it was here that the jury viewed the four bodies.[138-140]

Fox & Crown, Basford (1995)

Shortly after the crime on Tuesday 4th April 1837 Greensmith went to the village of Lambley and called at the Robin Hood public house, where he was well-known by the publican, John Brownley. He remained there all day but was arrested during the late evening, by the local parish constable who had received a description of a man who was wanted for murder. The next morning Greensmith was taken back to Basford to appear at the inquest during the afternoon of that day:

'At half-past twelve the coroner entered the Fox & Crown public house and a few minutes afterwards the yells, hooting and hissing of a dense crowd announced the arrival of the wretched culprit who was escorted into the jury room apparently unaffected by his awful situation. He was a tall man, healthy countenance with brown hair, light eyes with a degree of wildness about them and a peculiar formation of head, extremely long from the chin to the forehead. He was dressed in a blue waggoner's smock frock, silk handkerchief round his neck and heavy lace-up boots. His appearance was of great muscular power but there was nothing ferocious in his aspect and his countenance was rather that of mildness than otherwise. The rush to the room window to get a sight of the prisoner was tremendous so that several panes were broken and it was next to impossible for the constables to keep order.'

Coroner Swann questioned the prisoner as to his name and the names of the deceased children, which he readily answered. The jury of twelve men was then sworn and they left the jury room and proceeded to Greensmith's house to view the bodies. The crowd was very great but they readily made way for the coroner and jury to pass:

'On entering the room the whole of the four bodies immediately presented themselves, the eldest, John, in a small bed under the window, with his feet projecting from the bottom of the bedstead, the other three children lay in the larger bed. The livid hue of the skin, the swollen features and the discoloration round the neck evidently manifested great violence; it was a

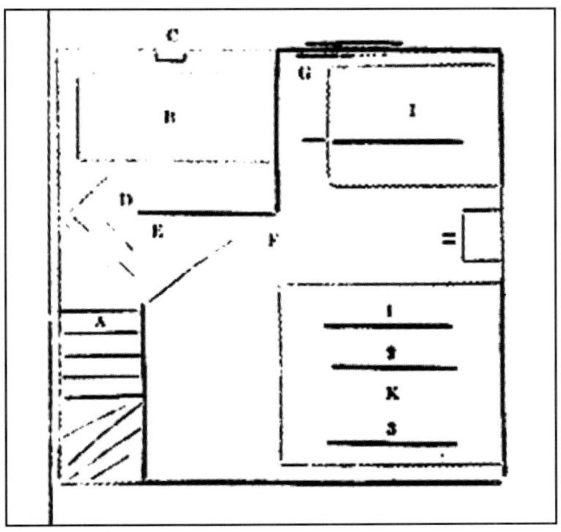

PLAN OF THE HOUSE IN WHICH THE MURDER TOOK PLACE

A Stairs from the lower room.
B The prisoner's room and bed.
C & D Window and door in the above
E Door to the children's room.
F Children's room.
G Window in the above.
H Fireplace.
I Bed and position in which John the eldest was lying with his feet out at the bottom.
K Bed in which the other three children were lying, 1 William, 2 Mark, 3 Ann.

revolting spectacle. There is reason to believe that the unhappy man, after perpetrating the murders, given in his own confession, closed the eyes of his innocent victims and probably laid them in the position in which they were found.'

A number of witnesses were carefully examined throughout the course of the proceedings and it transpired that Greensmith had some financial problems and that his landlord was pressing him for payment of rent that was due. He said that failure to meet his obligations would mean that his goods would be requisitioned. This possibly affected the prisoner's judgement. On closing the evidence the coroner asked the prisoner whether he wished to say anything to the jury but he would warn him that whatsoever he said would be taken down and produced in evidence thereafter. Greensmith then proceeded to give a detailed statement of his movements prior to the death of his children and admitted that he killed them:

'*Mr. Woodward asked me for the rent and I had told him that it was impossible for me to give it him next morning but I would give it him during the course of next week. He said he wouldn't be put off and that he'd have it or he'd take my goods and I thought that if he took my goods I should have ne'er a home nor nothing. I thought that sooner than have my children turned on to the street, I'd suffer what the law pleased to clap on me* [a buzz passed round the room among the jurors and spectators].'

In reply to questions by the coroner, Greensmith gave a very detailed description of how he strangled his children with his handkerchief and that he had no intention of ending his own life.

At the close the coroner said that in consequence of the full and ample confession by the prisoner it would be unnecessary for him to trouble the jury with any remarks, if they wished for a consideration he would have the room cleared. The jury thought it was not necessary and being all agreed a verdict of *Wilful Murder* was recorded against Thomas Greensmith, who was committed to take his trial at the Nottingham Summer Assizes.

His trial took place at the Shire Hall on Saturday 22nd July 1837 when he was found guilty of the wilful murder of his son, Mark Greensmith, and was sentenced to death by hanging.[141] However, this was later commuted to transportation for life and he was sent to New South Wales on the convict ship, Barosa[142] sailing on 4th August 1839 and arriving at Sydney on the 8th December 1839.[143] Although he had pleaded not guilty to the charge of the wilful murder of his son, he had previously at the coroner's inquest made a full confession of his crime. One may speculate that this confession may have influenced the authorities into saving him from the sentence of death.

(ii) Ann Saville and her children murdered by her husband, William Saville
[Table 8. footnote 8]

An inquest was held at the house of William Parr, constable at Colwick on Friday 24th May 1844 and by adjournment at the County Hall, Nottingham on Monday and Tuesday 27th and 28th May 1844. The subject of this inquiry was the murder of Ann Saville, aged 38 years, Harriet Saville, aged 7 years, Mary Saville, aged 5 years and Thomas Saville aged 3 years. William Saville the husband and the father of the three children was suspected of killing these four persons by cutting their throats:

County Hall, Nottingham (1833)

Previous to the inquest the police had detained Saville, *alias Nicholson*, in connection with the disappearance of his wife and family.[144] Blood had been found upon his trousers and one of his knees was marked as if he had knelt on wet grass and his boots bore marks of having been amongst grass and clay. He was remanded by the magistrates and taken to the House of Correction to await the inquest on the bodies that had in the meantime been found.[145]

'The morning being beautifully fine the roads from Nottingham to Colwick were literally lined with people anxious to catch a glimpse, if possible, of the wretched man charged with the commission of the awful crime of murder. But the carriage, in which the prisoner was conveyed being closed, no opportunity was afforded to the immense crowd of spectators. The prisoner was taken, handcuffed to a policeman, into Mr. Parr's house and thence to the barn to view the bodies. The jury were performing a similar ceremony. The prisoner on looking at them, burst into tears, and on being asked by the coroner if that was his wife and the others his children, he answered "yes".'

The evidence was then taken and the first witness was John Swinscoe, framework-knitter, of Carlton:

'About one o'clock yesterday (Wednesday) I found the bodies as I was going to get a little stuff for some rabbits, in a plantation adjoining the foot road leading from Carlton to Colwick. My son stood on the foot road while I went into the plantation; I saw three little children lying in the plantation as if they were asleep and I carefully went up to them, lest I should wake them. When I got to them, I thought they looked awkwardly and I rose on my feet to look over a child and perceived its eyes as if looking up. I immediately saw a wound in the throat of the child and blood on the whole of them. I ran and shouted to my son "Abraham, Abraham, what a shocking sight I have seen" and he went to look at them. He then went to fetch the constable, Mr. Parr, and I showed him where the three bodies lay and in four or five minutes he found the woman. I went up to her she was quite dead with her throat cut. She had a razor in her left hand.'

In his statement William Parr said that he removed the razor which was quite loose in Ann Saville's hand and she appeared to have been dragged through the weeds for about five yards from the bodies of the children. William Parr assisted by John Swinscoe removed the four corpses in a cart to a barn at Parr's residence where they lay on view for the jury.

The inquest was held over a period of three days and a large number of witnesses were closely examined. The coroner in summing up said the jury had now heard all the evidence in this long case and before they delivered their verdict he would read over the whole of the findings and make such comments, as he thought appropriate:

'This was certainly one of the most brutal and outrageous murders that had ever come under his notice and was perhaps unparalleled in the history of crime, at least that he knew of, in this county since he had the honour of being coroner. There was only one that he knew of that came anywhere near it and that was committed by Greensmith, of Basford, who murdered his own four children; but in this case it certainly was not so bad. There was none of the cruel spilling of human blood and though the jury had sufficient evidence that their lives had been taken there was the redeeming fact that Greensmith had made a full and free confession of his crime. In the current case there had been no confession but we had been lead to suppose that the murder had not been committed by the individual charged but by the unhappy woman herself, with the razor that was found in her hand. The case the jury had to decide was whether these murders were carried out by the woman herself or by some other person.'

After having heard evidence given by a number of witnesses, over the three days of the proceedings, the jury came to the conclusion that Ann Saville could not have killed her children. They concluded that all four persons died from the injuries received by the hand of William Saville. After deliberating for ten minutes, the jury arrived at a verdict of *Wilful Murder* against the prisoner, William Saville, who was sent to the County Gaol to take his trial at the next Assizes.

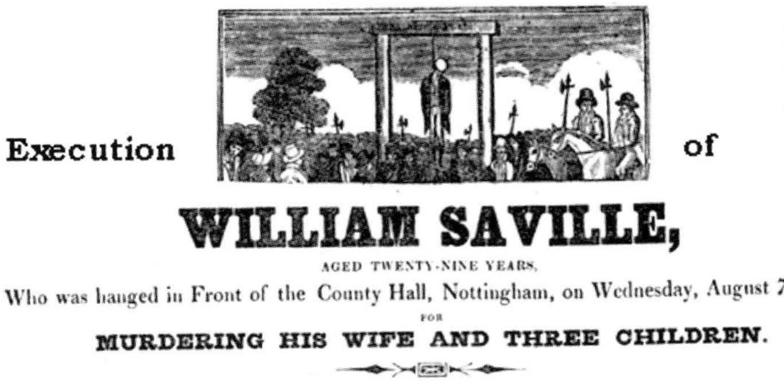
Execution of
WILLIAM SAVILLE,
AGED TWENTY-NINE YEARS,
Who was hanged in Front of the County Hall, Nottingham, on Wednesday, August 7, 1844,
FOR
MURDERING HIS WIFE AND THREE CHILDREN.

Section of a broadside printed by R. Sutton subsequent to the execution of William Saville (1844)

At his trial at the Nottingham Assize Court, Saville was convicted of the murder of his wife and three children and was sentenced to be hung.[146] His execution took place on Wednesday the 7th August 1844. It was a disastrous occasion for a number of onlookers were crushed to death during the melee of people outside the County Hall. In the absence of the Borough Coroner, Christopher Swann conducted the subsequent inquest on eight of the bodies. The verdict being that: '*the deceased individuals were accidentally thrown down, in and by a crowd of people, who had been attending a public execution in the town of Nottingham and were then and there trampled to death or suffocated.*'[147]

(iii) Joseph Barber murdered by Sarah Barber in cohort with Robert Ingram
[Table 8. footnote 11]

This notorious inquest on the body of Joseph Barber took place at the Sun Inn, Eastwood, over five days between the 24th March and 17th April 1851.[148-153]

Joseph Barber, aged 35 years, was a horse-dealer and coal-higgler and lived in comparatively comfortable circumstances. He had married Sarah Barber (née Banford Simpson) on the 29th April 1845 in the parish church at Eastwood when she was only seventeen. It appears that they had at times a tempestuous marriage and were frequently quarrelling. Apparently Joseph Barber was a notoriously bad character and according to one witness at the inquest he admitted, on his death-bed, '*that he was a swearing and drinking man and I hope the Lord will forgive me and have mercy on me*'. Robert Ingram, aged 19 years, (whose real name was Brierly or Bryley) had at one time been employed by Barber, appears to have assisted in the house; whether he was amorously involved with Sarah Barber is not certain. Although on the night of the 1851 census he was living at the same address in Eastwood.

Sun Inn, Eastwood (1876)

The most relevant evidence at the inquest, against the accused, was divided between:

i. The fact that Sarah Barber asked a number of persons to buy quantities of arsenic for her which she alleged was for disposing of mice.
ii. The analysis of the stomach and body tissues for the presence of arsenic.

'*William Simpson, plasterer of Spondon, being sworn said that I have lately been working at Eastwood and lodged at Mrs. Eley's. I remember that on Wednesday 19th March (the day before the deceased died), Mrs. Barber came to the house and asked her brother, George Simpson, who also lodged there, to fetch her a pennyworth of arsenic from Mr. Cullen's to poison mice. She gave him sixpence. She said that he must take a witness with him, for they would not let him have it without one, so I went with him. Mr. Cullen said to George "You must be careful with it, for there is as much as would poison two men." It was wrapped up and "Poison" was written on it. We were not away longer than ten minutes and when we returned Mrs. Barber was standing in the house. She put the package into her pocket but I advised her to wrap it in another paper, which she did and soon left the house.*'

Robert Ingram also later admitted to purchasing arsenic: '*A week since last Thursday night (as I believe) she sent me to fetch her a pennyworth of arsenic to poison mice with. I fetched it and gave it to her. There was the word "Poison" on the paper. That was the only time I ever fetched arsenic. She did not use it, but as it lay on the table she said to me "Robert I've taken a fresh thought – we'll not have any arsenic about now my husband is so ill," and she threw it into the fire.*'

The evidence of the medical practitioners following the analysis of the stomach and intestinal contents for the presence of arsenic was initially indeterminate. This was probably due to the lack of analytical skill on the part of some of the local surgeons and one (William Scott Smith) admitted, "*I was not confident of my own skill in analysing the stomach and I therefore called in the assistance of Mr. Wright.*" Although working together they were unable to detect the presence of arsenic. In the meantime Joseph Barber's brother had engaged a Mr. Robert Gossett Brown, a surgeon from Eastwood, to examine the contents of the stomach. He presented himself for examination but declined to give evidence unless he was admitted as a witness on behalf of the Crown. Christopher Swann expressed his willingness to hear him but initially objected to pay him out of the county funds. However, Mr. Brown informed him that both he and his brother, on separate occasions, had subjected the stomach contents of the deceased to a number of chemical tests. These analyses had detected the presence of arsenic. He then suggested his evidence should be heard and that a portion of the stomach should be sent either to Mr. Herapath of Bristol or Dr. Taylor of London, two of the most experienced analytical chemists in the country. Upon hearing this the coroner thought it was material that Mr. Brown's evidence should be taken:

' *I was present last Monday when the post-mortem examination was made but not when William Scott. Smith made an analysis of the contents of the stomach. I observed that the left lung was studded with a tuberculous deposit, as was also the apex of the right lung. About the pericardium there was some fluid. The muscular structure of the heart seemed exsanguined, the liver was rather larger and softer than was healthy; the gall bladder was full of bile and the general appearance of the bowels was ingested. The oesophagus was more vascular than normal. The appearance of the left kidney was not very healthy. The stomach and intestines I did not see opened but I saw them taken out by Mr. Smith and taken home. Mr. Smith favoured me with nine drachms of the fluid contents of the stomach. He also gave me the lower three inches of the oesophagus. ... At the commencement of the examination I asked to be allowed to look at the stomach when opened, but I heard nothing more about the matter until yesterday when I heard by chance that the stomach and intestines had been to Nottingham to be analysed. I met Mr. Smith yesterday who told me the result was unfavourable to the opinion that arsenic had been administered. Yesterday Mr. Smith gave me another small portion of the bowel. My brother and I took separate and distinct portions of the stomach and analysed them separately on Monday evening. Having put two drachms of the contents into a glass tube and added a little muriatic acid, I introduced into the tube some pieces of copper and applied heat. Having boiled it for some time over a spirit lamp I poured off the liquid when I found a deposit upon the bits of copper which I believed to be metallic arsenic. Having dried these bits I inserted them into a glass tube to which I applied gentle heat and on the glass tube I found deposited what I believe to have been crystals of arsenious acid. In order to prove as far as possible whether it was or not I added some distilled water and heated the contents over a spirit lamp. This solution was divided into two portions. To one I added ammonia nitrate of silver which yielded a yellow colour, to the other I added ammonia sulphate of copper by which the liquid changed to blue but on standing it turned green. The one precipitate I believe to have been the yellow arsenite of silver the other the green arsenite of copper. I went over the tests two or three times with the same result. My brother's results corresponded exactly with mine. The conclusion I draw from these tests is that there was arsenic present in the stomach and the system of the deceased. I would not pretend to swear positively that the deceased died from the effects of arsenic, but all the appearances found were such as I should expect to find would follow the administration of arsenic.*'

At the adjourned inquest Mr. Robert Gossett Brown, of Eastwood was further examined and said:

'*On Tuesday the 1st instant I took a portion of the oesophagus and cardiac region of the stomach and also a portion of the duodenum to Dr. Taylor at the chemical laboratory, Guy's Hospital and delivered them to him personally. They were the same portions, which I had received from Mr. Smith. I witnessed an analysis by Dr. Taylor of some of the mucous of the stomach, which proved beyond doubt the presence of arsenic. I also witnessed an analysis of a portion of the coats of the stomach, from which similar results were obtained. I am now fully convinced in my former opinion that arsenic was present in the stomach of the deceased. I have not the slightest doubt but that there was as much arsenic found as would destroy the life of a man. I left the contents that I took to Dr. Taylor with him.*'

The jury took 15 hours to arrive at the verdict that Sarah Barber, aged 23 years, was guilty of poisoning her husband, Joseph Barber, with arsenic and that Robert Ingram was an accomplice in causing his death. The jury had remained in consultation until half past eight o'clock when as was the custom:

'*not having arrived at a verdict they were locked up without fire, food or candle-light*'.

It appeared that the delay in reaching a decision was due to a less than satisfactory selection of jurors, for one of them was related by marriage to Sarah Barber. During the whole of the inquiry he seems to have acted more the part of a zealous advocate on her behalf rather than a juror.

By the time the inquest was held, Joseph Barber's death had already been registered and the cause of death was recorded as '*Rheumatic fever one month, diarrhoea four days.*'

At the subsequent trial at the Nottingham Assizes in July 1851 Ingram was acquitted of any crime but the guilt of Sarah Barber was confirmed. She was sentenced to death by hanging,[154] but this punishment was later commuted to transportation for life and was sent to Van Dieman's Land.[142] The vessel, the Anna-Maria, sailed from London on the 7th October 1851 arriving at Hobart on the 26th January 1852.[143] Sarah was one of 200 female convicts on the ship, four of whom died on the voyage. A newspaper report claimed that Barber was one of these[155] but this was not correct and in fact she remarried whilst in the antipodes.[156]

(iv) Mary Hallam murdered by John Jones [Table 8. footnote 6]

An inquest was initially held at the Ram Inn, Mansfield, on the 1st January 1842 but was adjourned to the Town Hall for greater convenience. The body in question was that of Mary Hallam, aged 19 years, who had been found by her father on the evening of the 30th December 1841 in a shoe-maker's workshop in the vicinity of Lister Lane, Mansfield. Her throat had been cut:[157]

House where the body lay (1842)

'*On Saturday morning, crowds assembled in the Market Place, to await the arrival of the coroner in the Champion Coach from Nottingham. When he and the reporters alighted they proceeded to the Ram Inn and a crowd of people who seemed highly excited followed them. The first step was to swear the twelve persons appointed as the jury. The coroner, jury and reporters then proceeded to view the body, which lay in the shop as it had been first found. On going up the stairs the sight was truly horrible – the body lay under the window, with several tremendous gashes in the throat, one actually extending from the left ear to the chin and another all across the throat to the length of six inches. The arms were stretched out and the sleeves and hands covered in blood. Her hair was in paper and the blood had covered her face and bosom and saturated her hair. Her eyes were staring open and with their glazed reflection gave a hideous finish to the distorted countenance. She was dressed in a brown print gown and had on black stockings and shoes.*'

PLAN OF THE INTERIOR OF THE ROOM AS IT APPEARED WHEN THE MURDER WAS DISCOVERED

A The stairs by which the room is entered, being the front of the house.
B The stalls on which the workmen sit to work, and had their tools.
D The window through which the father looked.
F The body, precisely as it lay, with blood all round it. The knife lay where the X is.
G Box of tools.
H Heap of rubbish in a corner.

On returning to the inquest room the jury having all taken their seats and the room having been filled with spectators the prisoner, John Jones alias Samuel Moore, was brought in and placed at the top of the table facing the coroner. He was a good-looking young man with dark hair, dark eyes, good nose and a large chin. The coroner then proceeded to examine a number of witnesses; it appears that Jones had formed an association with Mary Hallam but she was not inclined to encourage him. He confirmed that his name was Jones and not Moore, which he had assumed on his arrival in Mansfield, and that he was a 24-year-old cordwainer.

Sketch of John Jones

William Hallam, the father of Mary, made a long statement to the court in which he described in detail how he discovered the body of his daughter on that fatal evening:

'*William Hallam being sworn, deposed that he lives in Lister Lane and is a labourer. He has seen the body of his daughter. She was a single woman and would have been twenty years of age on the 19th of February next. She lived with the witness and he last saw her alive about one o'clock on Thursday. She did not dine with him but had just come home from a journey to visit her aunt in Worksop where she went on Christmas Day. The witness returned home from work about nine o'clock in the evening, which is his usual time and enquired about the whereabouts of his daughter. His wife told him she had recently gone out but as she was not wearing a bonnet or shawl she would not be long. About half past nine his wife went to a neighbour, Mrs. Skelton, but Mary was not there. Mr. Hallam went to look for her in the town but he could not find her. It was after eleven o'clock when he thought of going to the prisoner's workshop; Mrs. Ann Skelton accompanied him. He did not try the door but he put a chair on top of a table beneath the second storey, slid the window open and by the light of his lantern saw his daughter lying in all her blood upon the floor. She lay on her right side but mostly on her back. Her clothes were down a few inches from her shoes. They did not enter the room but went to fetch the constable, Mr. Mettham, and accompanied by the constable's nephew the three of them went to the prisoner's lodgings. The constable then took the prisoner to the lock-up. I went to fetch the surgeon, Mr. Hurt, he got out of bed and together with Mr. Mettham and Mrs. Skelton we entered the prisoner's workshop. We proceeded to go up the stairs and I saw my daughter lying on the floor in the same state as I had seen her through the window but I now saw the wounds in her neck. She appeared to be quite dead but I could not bear the sight and went away directly. I have not seen her since. I have known the prisoner for nearly two years. He usually goes by the name of Samuel Moore but I understand his proper name is John Jones. He was intimately acquainted with my daughter about nine months ago when he lodged at my house. He carried out a shoe-making business.*'

A number of other statements including those of the police and the surgeon were taken. After which coroner Swann proceeded to guide the jury in the consideration of their verdict. He could not find any single feature that could reduce the case to manslaughter and therefore they might dismiss that point from their minds, they would therefore have to consider who committed the murder. If they believed there was evidence enough, coupled with the statement of the prisoner, to send him for trial for wilful murder before a jury of his countrymen, they might do so. However, if they did not consider he was the man who committed the deed they must return a verdict of wilful murder against some person or persons unknown. He went over some parts of the evidence to show that the prisoner possessed an ill feeling towards Mary Hallam, which prompted him to carry out the deed. There was also convincing proof that Jones had previously made an attempt on her life. He also quoted other evidence to show that the prisoner must be the man by his knowledge of the position of the knife, the hiding place of the key and his ultimate confession of being the murderer. In addition there could be no doubt that the deceased died from the wounds she received from the clear and decisive evidence of the surgeon.

The room was then cleared and in a very short time the jury arrived at their verdict of wilful murder against the prisoner who was taken back to the Mansfield lock-up and transferred the following day to the County Gaol to await his trial at the next Assizes.

At his trial on the 12th March 1842 John Jones was found guilty of murdering Mary Hallam by cutting her throat with a shoe-maker's knife.[158] He was sentenced to death and was hung on the 23rd March 1842 in Nottingham.

(v) Murder by administering laudanum in a drink [Table 8. footnote 7]

An adjourned inquest was held on the 3rd March 1842 at the Pheasant public house in Radford on the body of Thomas Robinson, aged 70 years. He was a coal higgler residing at Radford. It appears from the testimony of persons who knew the deceased that he was a man of intemperate habits and had been accustomed to visit a brothel kept by Benjamin Hurd, aged 24 years, and his wife, Hannah, aged 23 years, situated in Bellfounder's Yard, Nottingham. Having disposed of a load of coal he went to this house on Friday 11th February 1842, where laudanum was given to him mixed with ale until he became insensible. He was then robbed of between 20 and 30 shillings, dragged down the stairs, taken out of the house and left in Parliament Street. He was later carried by a person, who knew him, into a stable and laid upon some straw and remained there all night. Apparently there was a copious discharge of brownish matter from his mouth. At six o'clock next morning he was still lying in the same position in which he had been left on the previous evening and appeared to be quite insensible, he neither spoke nor opened his eyes. About four o'clock in the afternoon he was taken home to Radford. Robinson's daughter said that she permitted her father to remain in the stable overnight, as he regularly got intoxicated and would come home at all hours when he had recovered and she thought this was a similar case. When he arrived home in the horse and cart, which she had sent to fetch him, he was then sensible but had to be assisted into the house. However, soon afterwards he again relapsed into insensibility and so continued until his death about mid-night. A witness who resided at the brothel gave details of the events which occurred whilst Robinson was in the house:[159]

Pheasant, Radford (1998)

'*That on going to my dinner I saw the mistress of the brothel, Hannah Hurd, pull a little bottle out of her bosom and pour the contents into an ale glass and fill it with ale. I said, "what's that stuff you're putting into the glass?" She replied, I've a man upstairs - I'm hocussing him.* [Hocussing - to stupefy with drugs for a criminal purpose – see Dickens Pickwick Papers 1837, xiii.] *At this time she gave the deceased about two tea-spoonfuls of laudanum. She returned downstairs and went up again two or three times, each time mixing a fresh glass of ale and laudanum until she had emptied the bottle, which was an ounce or a three-quarter ounce bottle. These doses not having the desired effect so soon as she wished, she fetched more ale and more laudanum and with this potent drug she kept plying her victim until she again emptied the bottle. When she was mixing ale and a portion of the second bottle of laudanum, she observed with all the coolness and depravity of heart which marked the infamous Burke and Hare, who were executed for a similar horrible offence, "this here will make six pennyworths he has had." Having again emptied the bottle, she placed it in her bosom. The impatience of this depraved female for the operation of the laudanum that she might commence plundering the wretched old man, appears to have been more like that of a demon than a human being. Having already given him, according to her own admission six pennyworth of laudanum she again went out of the house and returned in about five minutes, exclaiming, "this old man must go." She again went upstairs to give him another dose but the fatal effects of the laudanum had already taken effect. Robinson was drowsy and the fiend-like female put her arms round the waist of her victim and threw him on to the bed. He was shortly fast asleep and Hannah Hurd picked his pockets. With the money she fetched some clothes out of pawn and purchased wearing apparel.*'

The jury having considered this and the rest of the extremely voluminous evidence they returned a verdict of wilful murder against both Benjamin and Hannah Hurd and they were committed for trial.

At their trial at the Nottingham Summer Assizes on the 23rd July 1842, the counsel for the defence objected to the indictment. He said that as the poison was alleged to have been administered in the town of Nottingham and that the death had occurred in the county at large the coroner had exceeded his powers. The learned judge, however, over-ruled the objection as he said that the case came under the statute of 7 Geo. IV, c.64, s.12., which states that if a felony was begun in one county and completed in another the parties charged with committing the same could be tried in either. A number of witnesses were questioned about the events that had occurred on that fatal day in Bellfounder's Yard. Eventually the trial came to an end; initially the jury said that Hannah Hurd was guilty of administering the laudanum with intent to rob and not murder. After further guidance from his Lordship they declared that she was guilty of manslaughter. Her husband, Benjamin Hurd was acquitted. His Lordship said the jury had found Hannah Hurd guilty of the lesser crime, after a most patient trial. It would however be no escape for the prisoner – she would have to pass the remainder of her days in degradation, misery and wretchedness in a foreign land. He sentenced her to be transported for life.[160] She sailed on the 2nd October 1842, from Woolwich on the convict ship, Garland Rose,[142] which arrived in Hobart on the 20th January 1843.

(vi) The murder of George Shooter by his son Henry [Table 8. footnote 1]

George Shooter was a framework knitter, aged 53 years, residing at Sutton-in-Ashfield; he owned a number of stocking frames and he possessed a few acres of land. His son Henry, aged 19 years, had received a good education at the local non-conformist school and was currently apprenticed to a surgeon in Belper. It appears that he was making good progress in his chosen profession. However in the early hours of Tuesday 7th September 1830 he left his residence in Belper and walked to the family home at Sutton-in-Ashfield. Having entered the house he fatally stabbed his father with a surgeon's knife and shortly afterwards extinguished his own life with the same instrument. The inquest was held the next day at the Black Bull public house in the village. During the course of the investigation it emerged that there was a history of insanity in the family. This information possibly influenced the verdict of the jury who after a lengthy deliberation agreed that Henry Shooter being of unsound mind had killed his father and himself. They were buried during the evening of Thursday the 9th September 1830, in separate graves, at the parish church. There were some noisy scenes at the interment for it appears that there was some dissent at the verdict for it was believed that Henry Shooter was not insane and therefore he should have been denied a Christian burial.[161]

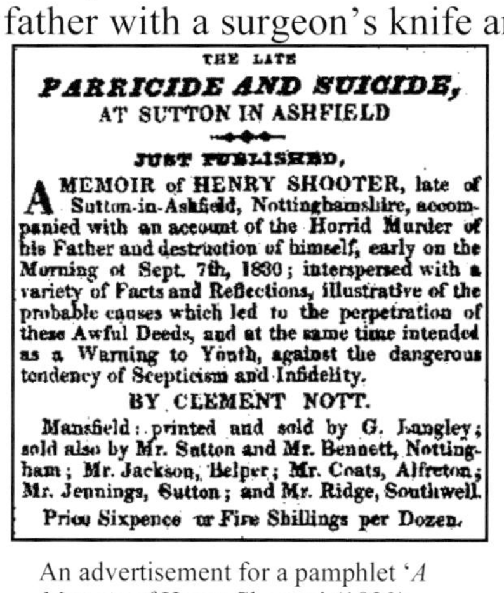
THE LATE
PARRICIDE AND SUICIDE,
AT SUTTON IN ASHFIELD

JUST PUBLISHED,

A MEMOIR of HENRY SHOOTER, late of Sutton-in-Ashfield, Nottinghamshire, accompanied with an account of the Horrid Murder of his Father and destruction of himself, early on the Morning of Sept. 7th, 1830; interspersed with a variety of Facts and Reflections, illustrative of the probable causes which led to the perpetration of these Awful Deeds, and at the same time intended as a Warning to Youth, against the dangerous tendency of Scepticism and Infidelity.

BY CLEMENT NOTT.

Mansfield: printed and sold by G. Langley; sold also by Mr. Sutton and Mr. Bennett, Nottingham; Mr. Jackson, Belper; Mr. Coats, Alfreton; Mr. Jennings, Sutton; and Mr. Ridge, Southwell.

Price Sixpence or Five Shillings per Dozen.

An advertisement for a pamphlet '*A Memoir of Henry Shooter*' (1830)

27. Manslaughter

During the 38 years of Christopher Swann's service as a coroner in Nottinghamshire, he presided over 35 inquests where the jury came to the conclusion that the deceased persons had, for a variety of reasons, met a violent death and their verdict was one of manslaughter. A list is given in Table 9. At the subsequent trials at the Nottingham Assizes the court did not uphold significant numbers of these coroners' verdicts and those originally apprehended were discharged. The sentences meted out to those found guilty varied from a fine of one shilling to transportation for life. In one instance the coroner's verdict was changed from manslaughter to murder and this person was sentenced to death by hanging but it appears that it was never carried out.

(a) The perpetrator was not identified

(i) Death from violence at Sneinton [Table 9. footnote 32]

'*An inquest was held at the Paul Pry, Sneinton, on Monday 11th January 1864 touching the death of a married woman named Mary Ann Barton, who was killed by violence inflicted by some person at present unknown. Elizabeth Barton said the deceased was the wife of Samuel Barton, who lives in Byron Square. She was 21 years old and had been married six years. On Saturday night I went out with her to look for her husband. As we were going along High Pavement a man who was passing in a state of drunkenness gave the deceased a blow with his elbow over the side which hurt her very considerably. She did not fall, but afterwards complained of pain. She called the man who struck her a "drunken brute", and said, "mind where you are going to". The man then turned round and used some very bad language, threatening what he would do to her. He appeared to be about 30 years old. He was very drunk and staggered as he went along. When we got to the corner of Mary Gate the deceased began to complain saying, "oh, what a pain I've got in my inside". When we came to Woolpack Lane she fell down and a gentleman who was passing picked her up. When we got home she was put to bed. I saw her on Sunday morning about 11 o'clock and on asking her whether she felt any better, she said she did not. She died later that day. I believe the blow given by the man has been the cause of her death. Edward Charles Buknall sworn, said I am a surgeon, living at Sneinton. I was called to see the deceased about 11 o'clock on Sunday morning and I attended at once. She complained of much pain in the lower part of her body, accompanied by vomiting. She was in quite a collapsed condition. About six o'clock I was called in hastily and I went at once but she was dead when I arrived. This afternoon I made a post-mortem examination of the body, Mr. Edward Wright and a friend being present at the time. We found the organs of the body in a healthy condition. There was a rupture that must have been caused by a heavy blow. The wound was very small and the haemorrhage must have been very gradual indeed. I should think after she received such a wound she would be able to walk home. The rupture could not be caused by natural means. The Coroner having summed up, a verdict of manslaughter against some person unknown was returned.*'[162] [The police were searching for the man who inflicted the injury.]

Table 9.

Inquests of Christopher Swann where the verdict was manslaughter

Place	Venue	Inquest date(s)	Deceased	Age *	Perpetrator (s)
Nottingham (Brewhouse Yard)	Gate	17.07.1828	William Oldham	54	George Skidmore [1]
Newthorpe	White Bull	07.09.1831	Sarah Bryan	1	John Dexter [2]
Sneinton	William IV	21.03.1833	Sarah Ann Lee	9m.	Ann Wilkinson [3]
East Bridgford	Royal Oak	24.08.1833	Mary Sissons	18	Francis Freer [4]
Mansfield Woodhouse	Parliament Oak	06.12.1835	William Huskinson	38	Person(s) unknown [5]
Mansfield	Old Eclipse	02.08.1836	Joseph Turner	n.r.	John Orton [6]
Lenton	White Hart	10.10.1836	Maria Castles	24	Henry Thos. Mortimer [7]
Selston	Bull & Butcher	27.12.1836	Isaiah Brierley	21	John Straw [8]
Mansfield	White Hart	06,08.06.1838	Thomas Chamberlain	25	James Kershaw [9] Thomas Clay [9]
Carrington	William IV	08,13.08.1838	Joseph Roberts	18	Richard Jackson [10] Thomas Gilbert [10]
Colston Basset	Martin's Arms	27.09.1839	John Lowe	33	Joseph Brooks [11]
Newthorpe	Ram	04,05.07.1842	Samuel Hallam	20	George Padley [12] John King [12] Richard King [12] Isaac Padley [12]
Carrington	William IV	16,18.08.1842	John Kirkwood	43	Thomas Mitchell [13]
Bulwell	house of Luke Houghton, beer seller	21,25.08.1845	Thomas Soar	36	Joseph Rollinson [14] William Longden [14]
Ruddington	Red Lion	15,17.08.1846	John / Seth Smith	n.r.	Henry Tyers [15]
Mansfield	Greyhound adjourned to the Town Hall	12.05.1849	Elizabeth Bailey	23	John Sansome [16]
Kirkby-in-Ashfield	Cricket Players	13,16.07.1849	Martha Wilkinson	12	William Atkinson [17]
Gotham	Cuckoo Bush	18,22.04.1850	George Yeomans	41	Thomas Swift [18]
Lenton	New Inn	11,13,14.11. 1851	James Handley	27	Thomas Walker [19]
Basford	Swan	04.05.1853	Horatio Trueman	12	Horatio Trueman sen. [20]
Mansfield	Yew Tree	07,08.04.1856	Samuel Buttery	13	Vincent Wood [21]
Nuthall	Red Lion	26,27,28.01. 1857	Henry Hinks	54	James Walters [22] William Walters [22]
Hyson Green	New Inn	04.05.1857	Mary Ann Hall	29	Sarah Watts *alias* Sarah Barrowdale [23]
Mansfield	Horse & Jockey	27.07.1857	George Bunting	75	William Lymer [24]
Daybrook	Black Swan	02.12.1858	Joseph Stevenson	n.r.	Henry Sulley [25]
Radford	White Lion	23.04.1859	Elizabeth/Eliza Conner	25	Dan Gilpin Thackeray [26]
Lowdham	Magna Charta	26.04.1861	James Watson	36	John Tuckwood [27] John Glazebrook [27]
Kirkby-in-Ashfield	Duke of Wellington	03.07.1861	Isaiah Allen	23	Thomas Heath [28]
Bulwell	Horse Shoe	10,16.09.1861	Christopher Williamson	21	Sarah Williamson [29]
Sneinton	Duke of Wellington	04,06.07.1863	William Fletcher	38	Joseph Patchitt [30]
Beeston	n.r.	06,07.08.1863	Elizabeth Oldham	2½	Bennett Carnell [31]
Sneinton	Paul Pry	11.01.1864	Mary Ann Barton	21	Person(s) unknown [32]
Stoke Bardolph	Ferry Boat	07,08.07.1864	Joseph Salvin	52	Henry Key [33]
Holme Pierrepont	Fox & Crown	10,11.09.1866	William Derry	42	Thomas Scott [34]
Bulwell	Scots Grey	16,19.11.1866	Thomas Leaper	41	Alfred Glover [35]

* n.r. = no record m. = months, other ages are given in years

Table 9. (cont.)

Notes or verdicts reached at subsequent trials

[1] George Skidmore ran over William Oldham with his cart but was found not guilty and discharged

[2] John Dexter ran over Sarah Bryan with his cart but was found not guilty of the charge and discharged.

[3] Ann Wilkinson left the child, Sarah Ann Lee, in a field with little clothing and exposed to the cold weather; she was found guilty and sentenced to transportation for life [report on page 74].

[4] Francis Freer was alleged to have been instrumental in causing Mary Sissons to fall down the stairs but no evidence was presented at his trial and he was consequently discharged.

[5] William Huskinson was run over by a horse and cart which failed to stop.

[6] John Orton was alleged to have killed Joseph Turner in a fight but was found not guilty and discharged.

[7] Maria Castles died in child-birth but Henry Thos. Mortimer, the accoucheur (obstetrician), was found not guilty of manslaughter but blameable for great neglect.

[8] John Straw was alleged to have wounded Isaiah Brierley and was found guilty but provoked and sentenced to 14 days in prison.

[9] James Kershaw was found guilty of killing Thomas Chamberlain in a fight and sentenced to six months in prison, Thomas Clay received three months for aiding and abetting.

[10] Joseph Roberts died in a road accident when two carts were racing; both Richard Jackson and Thomas Gilbert were found guilty but as there was no aggravation they were fined 1s. and discharged.

[11] John Lowe was killed by a blow with a pitch-fork but Joseph Brooks was found not guilty and released.

[12] George Padley, John King, and Isaac Padley were found not guilty of manslaughter in slaying Samuel Hallam in a fight but guilty of assault. John King was sentenced to four months in prison and George & Isaac Padley to three months. The case against Richard King was withdrawn.

[13] Thomas Mitchell was found guilty of killing John Kirkwood in a fight and sentenced to four months in prison with hard labour.

[14] Both Joseph Rollinson and William Longden were alleged to have allowed Thomas Soar to drown in a coal-pit but they were found not guilty and discharged.

[15] Henry Tyers was found not guilty of the manslaughter of John/Seth Smith and discharged.

[16] Elizabeth Bailey died through a miscarriage but whether it was caused by violence to her by John Sansome was not clear. He was however arrested and declared guilty of murder and sentenced to be hanged but it appears that this was never carried out and he was eventually released.

[17] William Atkinson was found guilty of killing his stepdaughter, Martha Wilkinson, by beating her and striking her on the head. He was sentenced to be transported for 15 years [report on page 74].

[18] Thomas Swift pleaded guilty to the charge of manslaughter of George Yeomans in a fight. He was fined 1s. and released.

[19] Thomas Walker was found guilty of striking and killing James Handley. He was sentenced to four months hard labour.

[20] Horatio Trueman senior was alleged to have deprived his son, Horatio Trueman, of sufficient food and that caused him to die of starvation. At his trial he was found not guilty of manslaughter and discharged.

[21] Vincent Wood pleaded guilty to accidentally shooting Samuel Buttery; he was fined 1s. and discharged.

[22] James and William Walters were found guilty of slaying Henry Hinks in a fight but as no weapons were involved they received a lenient sentence of one week in prison.

[23] A midwife, Sarah Watts *alias* Barrowdale, was found guilty of the manslaughter of Mary Ann Hall due to neglect at child-birth and sent to prison for 10 years.

[24] William Lymer was alleged to have struck George Bunting so causing his death. At his trial he was found not guilty and released.

[25] At the trial of Henry Sulley the jury found difficulty in coming to a unanimous verdict but eventually found him guilty of the death of Joseph Stevenson in a boiler explosion. He was given a lenient sentence of one further week in prison.

[26] A surgeon, Dan Gilpin Thackeray was found guilty of the death of Elizabeth/Eliza Conner by misuse of instruments when delivering her of a child. He was sentenced to 12 months in prison.

[27] As no evidence was given at the trial of John Tuckwood and John Glazebrook they were found not guilty of the death of James Watson in a fight [report on page 75].

[28] Thomas Heath was found guilty of the manslaughter of Isaiah Allen in a fight but because of his previous good character he was given a lenient sentence of two months imprisonment.

[29] Sarah Williamson killed her brother, Christopher Williamson, by throwing a bobbin at him. She appears to have been spared coming to trial.

[30] Joseph Patchitt was found not guilty of killing William Fletcher in a fight.

[31] Bennett Carnell was found not guilty of shooting Elizabeth Oldham.

[32] Mary Ann Barton was attacked in the street and died from internal injuries [report on page 71].

[33] Henry Key was found not guilty of stabbing Joseph Salvin in the eye.

[34] Thomas Scott was found not guilty of the manslaughter of William Derry in a fight and discharged.

[35] Alfred Glover was found not guilty of the manslaughter of Thomas Leaper by striking him with a poker and he was discharged.

(b) The perpetrator was known and sent for trial at the Nottingham Assizes

(i) The tragic death of Sarah Ann Lee of Sneinton [Table 9. footnote 3]

'*An inquest was held on the 21st March 1833 at the sign of the William IV public house in Sneinton upon the body of Sarah Ann Lee, aged nine months. Her mother, Ann Lee, had left the child in the charge of a 10-year old girl, Caroline Blagdon, who took her out for a walk. They met a person called Ann Wilkinson, in a field near Nottingham, who partly stripped the baby of her clothes, which included her frock, pinafore, shoes and socks, and left her exposed to the cold weather with the result that the little girl died later of exposure. The coroner's jury was satisfied that Ann Wilkinson caused the child's death and returned a verdict of manslaughter against her.*'[163] At the trial of Ann Wilkinson she was sentenced to transportation for life for stealing the child's clothes[164] and later sent to New South Wales penal colony.'[142]

King William IV, Sneinton (1998)

(ii) The violent death of Martha Wilkinson of Kirkby-in-Ashfield [Table 9. footnote 17]

'*An inquest was held on the 13th July and by adjournment on the 16th July 1849 at the Cricket Players Inn, Kirkby-in-Ashfield, upon the body of Martha Wilkinson, aged 10 years. She was the daughter of the wife of William Atkinson prior to her marriage to Atkinson. On the 12th July Martha Wilkinson was assisting her stepfather to hoe turnips. The day was very hot and she had difficulty in keeping up with Atkinson and he threatened her and struck her across her back with his hoe. A fellow worker told him not to be so cruel and begged him not to hit her with such an unlawful weapon. He had struck her again and she said "Oh, don't, father, I will try my best to do the work." He struck her six or seven times afterwards with the hoe shaft about the back and shoulders and the last blow he gave the child broke the hoe into two pieces. He then broke off an ash stick and when she got behind with her work again he again hit her over the shoulders and head. The witness said "Don't be so foolish as to hit her over the head". She seemed frightened and kept saying, "Oh father let me go home" and complained that her head hurt her. The witness said I could not bear it any longer and told her to go home which she did – it was about 11 o'clock. We left work about six o'clock, when we had passed three fields we came across Martha Wilkinson lying by the side of the hedge – she was dead. A post-mortem examination was made and very extensive bruises were found on different parts of the head. The medical opinion was that these injuries had been the cause of death. The verdict was one of manslaughter against William Atkinson.*'[165, 166]

Man assaulting a woman (1861)

At the trial of Atkinson in March of the following year the judge said: '*After the child made repeated appeals to your paternal feelings and after you had been remonstrated with by your brother-in-law you still persisted with that inhumane punishment. It is manslaughter of a very aggravated character, juries of former times would undoubtedly have arrived at a verdict of wilful murder, but nevertheless you must receive a very heavy punishment. You will be transported beyond the seas for the period of 15 years*.'[167]

(iii) A man killed at Lowdham in a fight [Table 9. footnote 27]

A shocking case of death from violence took place at Lowdham on the morning of Wednesday the 24th April 1861. The name of the deceased was James Watson a framework knitter aged 36 years. At the inquest held on view of the body at the Magna Charta public house on the following day, witnesses from the village were examined:

'Harriet Watson, widow of the deceased said when her husband finished work on the evening of the 23rd he obtained his wages and went to the White Lion public house. At half-past eleven o'clock she went to this inn to fetch him home but he told her that he was not yet ready. She remained there until 12 o'clock and by this time he was in a very intoxicated state. There were with him, John Glazebrook, John Brown, Thomas Parkes, Joseph Bagguley, John Tuckwood, Elias Deabill and George Keeley. About one o'clock I went out again to fetch him home but found him lying in the street quite speechless. John Glazebrook was putting his clothes on having stripped to fight her husband. Two men assisted her to carry her husband to his house and laid him on the floor, there was a bloody discharge coming from his nose. He did not recover consciousness and was dead by the next morning. After his death she sent for Mr. Day, surgeon and saw a large lump on the back of her husband's head.'

Magna Charta, Lowdham (1993)

This was clearly a public house brawl that spilled out into the main street in Lowdham, and there were a number of persons drinking and milling about at this late hour. From the evidence presented to the court over the two days of the hearing it seems that two contenders, John Glazebrook and John Tuckwood, were according to the jury, the culprits who had struck the blows that resulted in Watson's death. They were committed on a charge of manslaughter to appear at the Nottingham Assizes.[168] However at their trial no further evidence was presented and the charge was dismissed.[169]

28. Homicide

Coroner Swann presided over two inquests in which the jury returned verdicts of homicide, in the first it was recorded as being justifiable. In the second, held some years later, it was deemed homicide by misadventure:

(a) Justifiable

An election riot in Nottingham (1865)

'An inquest was held on the 22nd December 1832 at the King & Miller, Mansfield, on view of the body of Edmund Poole, aged 18 years. On the previous Wednesday afternoon the poll for the election of Members of Parliament to

represent the North Division of the County of Nottingham closed; at this stage a mob of people had gathered and they were hooting and shouting. As night drew on the violence of the mob increased and a great number of stones were thrown into the Swan Inn yard and some panes of glass were broken. Eventually the Riot Act was read in the Market Place and the special constables were turned out and endeavoured to disperse the people. It appears that the deceased, Edmund Poole, was in the crowd but from witness statements he was not taking a very active part. He was struck on the head by a constable wielding his staff, but at the inquest this person could not be reliably identified. Poole walked home and as he had a severe pain in his head went to bed but he died early on the following morning. A surgeon had visited him and reported that the deceased was excessively cold, he was insensible and had a bruise on the left side of his head. A post-mortem was carried out which showed that there was a considerable amount of blood in the sinuses of the brain that would have been the cause of death. A blow from a blunt instrument would most likely cause such an injury. The jury returned a verdict: Justifiable Homicide.'[170]

(b) Misadventure

'*An inquest was held on the 2nd and by adjournment on the 6th April 1852 at the Crown & Anchor, Mansfield, on the body of Elizabeth Hollingworth, aged 49 years. On the night of Saturday 20th of March a dispute arose in the family between her husband and one of their married sons who was living in the house with his wife and child. In the course of an argument her husband struck his son but Elizabeth Hollingworth intervened by placing herself between the two to prevent further blows, but her husband pushed her to one side. She fell to the ground and her two other sons took her into the house as she was complaining of a severe pain in her head. Medical assistance was obtained and as she was suffering from concussion her head was shaved. She remained insensible for several days but later she recovered although this was of a short duration and she again lost consciousness until she died. After due consideration of the facts of the case, the jury arrived at the conclusion that her husband had been the unintentional cause of the poor woman's death and therefore returned a verdict: Homicide by misadventure.'*[171]

Crown & Anchor, Mansfield (1998)

29. Unusual verdicts

There were a number of verdicts that appear to be rather bizarre. Today's coroner will have access to sophisticated medical and forensic facilities so assisting him to arrive at the most likely cause of death. His nineteenth century predecessors were of course denied these advantages. It must also be appreciated, that as we do not have sight of Coroner Swann's original depositions, we are therefore dependent on the interpretation of the facts by newspaper journalists. They may possibly have included a little more sensationalism to the proceedings of the inquest in order to give the report greater appeal to their readership:

Death from excessive eating '*An inquest was held on the 5th February 1866, at the White Hart, Arnold, touching the death of James Chettle, 64 years old. He obtained his living by going about the country dressing mill-stones. From the evidence of Thomas Broomhead, it seems that the deceased, on Friday night, was lodging at Mr. Breffits, at Slothorne, Arnold, and was seen about eight o'clock*

White Hart, Arnold (1964)

eating a large carrot, weighing about a pound. The deceased went to bed about nine o'clock, and had been there for about half an hour when he complained of being short of breath. He then got up and tried hard to breathe more freely. When asked what he had eaten he said "a carrot, two pounds of onions, together with a pound of pig's fry". He came downstairs and was given brandy but he continued to groan and froth at the mouth. He remained sitting in a chair until he died, shortly after 11 o'clock. The jury returned a verdict: That the deceased died from overloading his stomach, by eating to excess.'[172]

Death from eating ox-tail soup '*An inquest was held on the 5th January 1858, at the Nag's Head, Mansfield, touching the death of Mary Machin, three years old. Her mother, said that last Thursday she purchased six pennyworth of ox-tail, of which she and her family partook on Friday and felt no evil effects. On Saturday afternoon she brought out the pan in which it was cooked, intending to make soup of the liquor, but perceiving that it smelt rather sour, she said in the presence of the children, that she would give it to the pigs. Shortly afterwards she went upstairs, leaving the pan on the table and cautioning her children against touching it. On coming down she found that her son, Henry, aged eight years, and the deceased had drunk a quantity of the liquor between them. In a short time the two children became ill and complained of pains in their stomachs. Dr. Donovan, assistant to Messrs. Cooper & Godfrey, surgeons, came to see them and he administered emetics and the boy vomited freely and recovered. Unfortunately the little girl continued to get worse and died in the evening. Donovan deposed that he had examined the remaining ox-tail liquor, but not minutely. He tested it for arsenic and antimony but did not find any. He also gave some of the liquor to a dog and it had no ill effects on the animal. Verdict: That the child, being of a weak constitution, took some "ox-tail soup" which caused its death.*'[173]

Death from fear and excitement '*An inquest was held on the 14th July 1856, at the house of W. Parr, farmer, Colwick, on the body of William Tacey, aged 13 years. It appears that on Sunday evening whilst running away from a group of lads who were chasing him and his companions, he complained of feeling ill and fell to the ground. He was very frightened and said he was afraid the other lads would catch him and beat him. He breathed twice very heavily and expired. Mr. Davison, surgeon, said that the deceased was subject to epileptic fits and was suffering from disease of the heart. He was of the opinion that he died from fear and extreme excitement, the result of over-exertion in running. Verdict accordingly.*'[174]

Death from fright '*An inquest was held on the 17th June 1844, at the White Lion, Beeston, on the body of Louisa Brown, aged five years. Last Friday, the deceased and a friend, another little girl, went to visit her uncle, and when they knocked on the door it caused his dog to bark. When her cousin opened the door the dog rushed after the children who ran away but it caught hold of the deceased's clothes and pulled her down, her head hit the ground and her bonnet was crushed. The dog did not bite her. Her cousin lifted her up and asked if she was hurt and she said "no" but she could not stand. Her uncle took her into his house when she began to be sick and vomited. She was later taken home but she continued to be sick and also convulsed but no medical help was obtained. Her aunt went to see her on Saturday morning and found her dying but before a surgeon arrived she died. Verdict: Died from the effects of fright by a dog and the jury were of the opinion that proper medical aid should have been sought earlier.*'[175]

30. Died in a chapel or in a church

There are a few inquests following the sudden death of persons while they were in a place of worship; this appears to make a verdict that death was due to '*the sudden visitation of God*' very appropriate!

Death in a Methodist chapel at Newthorpe '*An inquest was held on the 25th April 1837 at the Ram Inn, Newthorpe, on the body of Elizabeth Purday, aged 43 years. Rebecca Saxton deposed that on Sunday night, I was at the New Methodist chapel, at Hill Top and the deceased was also there and sat about two seats in front of me. Her daughter, 18 years of age was sitting in the gallery. About half past seven o'clock, just as the minister was finishing his sermon, the deceased's daughter fainted and some persons brought her down. Whilst they were carrying the daughter out of the chapel, I saw the deceased's head falling backwards, as she sat upon her seat. I immediately went to her but before I reached her, her head fell back again and she died immediately. Her husband had gone to preach at Codnor Park that evening. Verdict: Natural death by the sudden visitation of God.*'[176]

Parishioners listening to a sermon (1855)

Death in the parish church at Gedling '*An inquest was held on the 27th December 1865 at the Chesterfield Arms, Gedling, over the body of Samuel Reed, aged 84 years. For the last four or five years he had been a communicant at Gedling church. About half past twelve on Christmas day he left home to receive the Holy Sacrament and was observed resting himself two or three times on the way. The Parish Clerk saw him enter the church and go into his pew. As the clerk could not see the old man in the pew he believed he was kneeling in prayer, which was his usual habit. However, in a minute or so he heard the sound of a fall and going to the pew saw the deceased lying on his face on the floor. He raised him up but he neither breathed nor stirred and it was then found he was dead. The verdict of the jury was: Dropped down dead in church from natural causes, by the sudden visitation of God.*'[177]

31. Inquests associated with the Union Workhouses at Basford, Bingham, Gedling, Mansfield, Radford or the General Lunatic Asylum in Sneinton or the General Hospital and the County Gaol in Nottingham

Ninety-five out of every hundred inquests taken by Christopher Swann were held in public houses or beer houses. Whilst this book focuses primarily on these principal venues, for the sake of completeness it is worthwhile to make mention of some of the other groups. These were the workhouses (sometimes referred to as "houses of industry") situated in the coroner's district or the Nottingham General Lunatic Asylum located in Sneinton or the General Hospital or County Gaol. Not all the deaths of their luckless inhabitants reported to the coroner would be investigated there for sometimes the inquest was held in a nearby public house. It may also be noted that a workhouse occasionally served as a convenient venue for an inquest on a person who had died nearby:

(a) The Union Workhouse at Basford

Child dies after being washed with cold water '*An inquest was held on the 27th January 1832 at the House of Industry, Basford, on the body of John Burton, a male bastard child aged four days. It was found dead in the room with his mother and had recently been washed with cold water and as it had been healthy before washing, the surgeon could find no other causes for his death. There were no marks of violence on the body. Verdict: Died in consequence of being washed in cold water by Maria Morton.*'[178]

The outcome of the following inquest, held not in a workhouse but in a local hostelry, on the body of John Parkes was very disturbing. In retrospect, it is most unlikely that Coroner Swann could have anticipated that it would become the focus of national debate in the House of Commons during the passage of the Poor Law Continuation Bill of 1841. It is said that it even persuaded Sir Robert Peel that the Boards of Guardians required supervision and guidance, strengthening his belief in the principle of centralisation and helped to prolong the existence of the Poor Law Commission:

The death of a very ill pauper who had been taken from Stoke Barcolph to Basford '*An inquest was held on Wednesday 27th and Friday 29th January 1841 at the sign of the Pear Tree, Basford, touching the death of John Parkes, aged 45 years. James Johnson, master of the Union Workhouse, said that the deceased was brought to the workhouse in the afternoon of the previous Monday by two men in a cart with a written order which read: "Please take in John Parkes that is all" W. Gill overseer, Stoke. The deceased was in a very bad state of health, he could not walk and was carried from the cart to the sick ward. The two men said he had a very bad leg and was very ill, they brought no message with the order. Later that day Mr. Morley, surgeon to the Union, saw him but little could be done for him and he died the next day. From the evidence it seems that whilst the surgeon responsible for the Parish of Stoke Bardolph had seen John Parkes once, but he refused on the request of the overseer to examine him prior to him being taken to the Basford Workhouse. Other witnesses were of the opinion that he was not in a fit condition to travel the nine miles, a journey taking 1½ hours. The weather on that day was exceedingly cold and the Union Surgeon told the Workhouse Master of the cruelty and impropriety of sending a man that distance exposed to the inclemency of the weather, especially as the deceased was in a dangerous state. After a long and detailed examination the jury arrived at their verdict that John Parkes died from exhaustion and exposure to cold and was suffering from inflammatory erysipelas. They were also of the opinion that Sanford Tatham Davison, the surgeon, and William Gill, the overseer, were guilty of neglect in their respective duties towards the deceased and were highly censurable. It also appeared to the jury that the deceased did not receive that care, diet and attention after he was brought into the workhouse, which he so urgently required.*'[179]

Pear Tree, Basford (1998)

Accidental death in the workhouse from a gunshot wound '*An inquest was taken on 9th September 1831 at the Horse & Jockey, Basford, on view of the body of William Bettison, aged 60 years. It appears that the deceased, who was an old soldier and fought at Waterloo, had been an inmate of the poorhouse for some months. On the morning of the Coronation* (of William IV)*, the governor of the house of industry and the deceased with some other paupers were in a hovel near the house, preparing various firearms to be discharged in the rejoicing. The deceased took a blunderbuss, which was charged with powder only, and when holding the butt against his body it suddenly went off, punching him very violently. He was taken to his room in great pain, he was bled by the surgeon and given proper medicines but he died* *the following morning. It appeared that the thump of the gun had ruptured some of his bowels and injured the anterior lobe of the liver. Verdict: Accidental death.'*[180]

(b) The Union Workhouse at Bingham

Considerable excitement occurred at Bingham during the first week of December 1852 in consequence of an inmate of the workhouse having confessed to suffocating her illegitimate child (Table 8. footnote 13). The child had been born on the 24th November but the mother, Mary Ann Parr, constantly refused to suckle it and the child died on Friday 3rd December:

Murder in the workhouse *'An inquest was held in the workhouse on the 4th December 1852 but adjourned until the 7th so that a post-mortem on the body of the child could be carried out. The surgeon said that he had no doubt that the child had died from the exclusion of air from the lungs. Mary Ann Parr, aged 25 years, was brought before the coroner and made the following statement – I did smother the child against my breast on purpose to take away its life and when I found it was dead I became affrighted. I was not exactly sure it was dead till my mistress came and told me..... Thomas Carnell of Bingham, a tailor, is the father of my child and I have nothing further to say. The jury then returned a verdict of wilful murder against her and the coroner thereupon issued a warrant for her committal to the Assizes.'*[181]

At her trial Mary Ann Parr was found guilty of murdering her child and sentenced to death but this was later commuted to transportation, but being of unsound mind she was sent to Broadmoor.[182]

(c) The Union Workhouse at Gedling

Coroner Swann held one inquest at this Workhouse situated on the corner of Stoke Lane and Burton Road. The deceased was not an inmate but had been involved in an accident nearby:

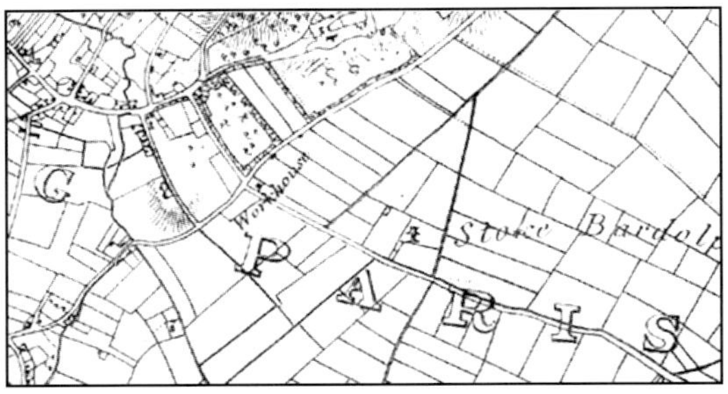

Site of the Gedling Workhouse (1835)

Accidental death *'An inquest was held on the 4th May 1830 at the Gedling House of Industry on view of the body of Thomas Barlow, aged 17 years, a native of Little Warsop. It appears that the deceased together with Jesse Smith, farming man to Mr. Scorer, of Scarcliffe, Derbyshire, had gone on the 3rd May to Stoke Bardolph for a load of pigeon-dung. On their return, while passing Gedling Workhouse, the deceased was walking too near the waggon; when turning round to speak to Smith, the wheel caught his foot and he was dragged down and the wheels passed over his chest. He was taken into the house and medical aid was obtained but he died in less than two hours. Verdict: Accidental death, with a deodand of 1s. on the wheel.'*[183]

(d) The Union Workhouse at Mansfield

A child falls into a cauldron of hot broth in the workhouse kitchen *'An inquest was held on the 18th July 1845 at the sign of the Wheatsheaf in Mansfield, on view of the body of Fanny Radford aged nine years. Etty Yates aged 11 years said I am a pauper in the Union Workhouse at Mansfield and knew the deceased who was also a pauper in the same house. On Wednesday afternoon last about one o'clock I saw the deceased at dinner with the rest of us and afterwards we went into the yard to play and then we went into the school. Some three minutes later I heard a scream coming from the cooking house and I ran there immediately and I saw the deceased in one of the coppers which was about three parts full of hot broth. I took hold of her shoulders and lifted her out on to the copper top, Mrs. Lindley, who is the mistress and overlooker of the children, lifted her down. I saw her when she was stripped, she was scalded up to the middle of her body. We sometimes get hot water out of the copper and I suppose she had gone with a bucket to do the same. I can reach the copper without climbing on to it but the deceased could not. The cooking house is in the play yard and when it is not in use the door is locked. The little girls are forbidden from going into the cooking house and have been beaten on previous occasions for doing so. Fanny Radford was put to bed and was under the care of the surgeon but she died in the evening of the same day. Verdict: Died as a result of being accidentally scalded. The jury was of the opinion that the cooking house was in a dangerous situation and recommended that the Board of Guardians should either remove it to some safer place or protect it from access to children.'*[184]

Wheatsheaf, Mansfield (1970)

Death from severe burns in the workhouse kitchen *'An inquest was held on the 22nd June 1850 at Mansfield Union Workhouse, upon the body of a pauper named Sarah Johnson, aged 41 years. From the evidence of James Nicholson, governor of this house, the deceased was admitted on the 2nd May 1844 and had continued to live there ever since. On Monday the 10th June Mr. Nicholson heard loud screams coming from the women's apartments and on hurrying there he found the deceased enveloped in flames. He managed to extinguish the flames with the aid of a carpet. She was very much burnt on her hands, arms, neck and face and she was put to bed. Despite every attention paid to her by the surgeon she gradually got worse and died ten days later. It seems that she had gone into the cooking room, without any authority to do so, and set herself on fire whilst getting some hot water from the copper. The jury returned a verdict: Died in consequence of being accidentally burnt.'*[185]

(e) The Union Workhouse at Radford

Death from smallpox in the workhouse *'An inquest was held on the 27th July 1854 and by adjournment on the 2nd August at the Radford Union Workhouse on the body of Elizabeth Rosling who had died of an attack of smallpox in the workhouse. The deceased had been in service in Nottingham and when the disease manifested itself she was removed to a friend's house in Ison Green and from there to the workhouse. As the case originally appeared there were some rather suspicious circumstances but these were satisfactorily explained during the adjournment. Verdict: That the deceased died a natural death from natural causes to wit, from smallpox.'*[186]

Death of a young girl in the workhouse *'An inquest was held on the 25th February 1844 at the Radford Union Workhouse to enquire into the cause of death of Ann Jane Foston. The deceased was six years of age and one of the children of Sergeant Foston, who died in a hospital at Palmalee, in the East Indies. Her mother died in Liverpool Workhouse in 1841 and the following year the deceased and her sister, Elizabeth Foston, aged 12 years were* *removed to Radford Workhouse. Last Friday the deceased had a headache and complained of feeling cold when she went to bed. Her sister asked another girl, Sarah Townsend, to sleep with her which she did. About two o'clock in the morning Sarah Townsend got out of bed and woke Elizabeth Foston telling her that her sister's hands felt cold and then they found that the child was dead. The Matron of the Workhouse was called but of course she could do nothing. After a post-mortem examination, Dr. Lightfoot gave it as his opinion that death had been occasioned by a convulsive fit produced by congestion of the brain. The deceased had been under medical treatment the greater part of the time she had been in the workhouse. Verdict: Death from natural causes, to wit, congestion of the brain.'*[187]

(f) The General Lunatic Asylum in Sneinton

The foundation stone of this extensive and well-constructed public building was laid on the 31st May 1810 and was opened for the admission of its unfortunate inmates on the 12th February 1812. It was situated in the parish of Sneinton so that it lay within the district overseen by Coroner Swann and during the period of his tenure he held several inquests within the precincts of this building. Of these there were a number of cases of suicide and two of these are highlighted below:

County Lunatic Asylum, Sneinton (c.1818)

Death of a patient by jumping out of a window at the asylum *'An inquest was held on the 31st March 1854 at the County Lunatic Asylum, Sneinton, over the body of James Acton Donaldson. The deceased was 39 years old and was a civil engineer by profession. Latterly he became subject to great excitability and for the benefit of his health he had been staying with Mr. Redfern, farmer, of Thrumpton. He expressed to this person a great horror of self-destruction and begged him to take charge of two razors for him. He continued to get worse and had a great propensity to throw himself out of a window. He was admitted to the asylum on the 29th February and consigned to the care of an attendant named William Townsend. This person stated that on Thursday morning, Mr. Donaldson was walking down the gallery and he was in his room at the end. Witness had been serving something to a patient and while his back was turned the deceased entered the apartment and he heard him scuffling against the chair under the window. Immediately dropping the pot he was holding Townsend made an unsuccessful attempt to catch hold of his legs as the unfortunate gentleman was in the act of throwing himself out of the window. He immediately went below and found the deceased lying on his back. His brains were scattered about, his head having hit the lower window-sill in his fall. He breathed slightly but died in a few seconds. Verdict: That the deceased, being a lunatic, was accidentally killed by throwing himself out of a window at the asylum.'*[188]

Death of a patient by hanging and suffocation *'An inquest was held on the 12th March 1858 at the lunatic asylum, Sneinton, upon the body of John Clarke, a private lunatic patient. The deceased was a farmer and resided at Selston. He was received into the asylum on the 4th December 1857, labouring under a suicidal mania. Before leaving home, he had made three attempts to kill himself. On the previous Wednesday Dr. Stiff saw him in one of the galleries reading Arabian Night's Entertainments, and shortly afterwards an assistant who had only been away from him for 20 minutes found him on the staircase quite dead. He had tied his handkerchief to a steam pipe and suffocated himself by kneeling down on the stairs. The jury returned a verdict accordingly.'*[189]

(g) The General Hospital in Nottingham

The General Hospital was founded in 1780 and built on land given by the Corporation of Nottingham and also by the Duke of Newcastle. Whilst the major part of the building was in the Borough of Nottingham it appears that some of it was erected on land which was in the Liberty of the Castle.[190] This latter area being an extra-parochial district was not within the jurisdiction of the "town" but included within the county. There were many inquests held in the General Hospital on persons who had died therein and in the vast majority of instances these came under the aegis of the Borough Coroner. However, a few inquests were held by Christopher Swann in this building and one can only presume that these individuals had died in that part of the hospital that would have been on land under his authority. The situation appears to be similar to that which appertained at the Trent Bridge Inn where the boundary of the borough and county bisected this public house (see page 18). This is a typical example of an inquest in the General Hospital:

General Hospital, Nottingham (1782)

Death of a patient who was admitted into hospital suffering from a fever '*An inquest was held on Sunday 7th January 1838, at the General Hospital in the Liberties of the Castle, on view of the body of Mary Priestley. Mr. F. Sibson, resident surgeon, stated that the deceased went into the hospital on the 20th December, labouring under fever. She was admitted under the care of Dr. Howitt and had received such treatments, as he (Dr. H.) considered her case demanded; she went on gradually improving. However on Friday morning a nurse informed Mr. Sibson that Mary Priestley was dead; he went to see her immediately, she was lifeless, her heart having ceased to beat and her face had become pale. Yesterday afternoon her body was opened and examined by the witness; there was found to be an enlargement of the heart and dropsy of the heart bags, marks of inflammation in the bowels, indicating ulcerations from fever. These were healing but the bowels were turned one part into the other, the blood of the heart was perfectly fluid, from which appearance he inferred that death was purely sudden. He was not surprised at sudden death occurring to a subject labouring under such circumstances. The night and day nurses were both examined and stated that every attention had been paid to her. Verdict: Natural death from natural causes.*'[191]

(h) The County Gaol in Nottingham

The Nottinghamshire County Hall, sometimes referred to as the Shire Hall and the adjacent County Gaol on High Pavement, has a long history stretching back into mediæval times.[192] The old Hall was demolished and a new building opened for judicial purposes in 1772 and it is this venue that would have been familiar to Coroner Swann. It was incumbent on the prison authorities to notify him of any deaths of inmates under their charge that occurred. From reports in the local press he officiated on 14 occasions on the deaths of prisoners who had died in the County Gaol, the inquests being held in County Hall. These are two examples:

Death of a person imprisoned for being in debt *'On Sunday 6th January 1833 an inquest was taken by Christopher Swann at the County Hall on view of the body of William Mell. He was being confined in prison for the reason that he owed two of his cousins £275 9s. From the evidence of the jailer it appears that Mell had been unwell for three or four months. On Friday evening he had been with other prisoners in their day room and was in good spirits and sang several songs. On Saturday morning he complained of feeling unwell and the jail surgeon immediately attended, ordered him to bed and sent medicines but he died about noon on that day. Mr. G. M. White opened the body and attributed his death to cramp of the stomach. Verdict: Natural death.'*[193]

Death of a man due to be transported *'On Friday 5th March 1852 an inquest was held at the County Gaol on the body of John Ord, aged 26 years. Mr. George Wright Hildyard deposed that on the 16th August 1851 the deceased was imprisoned on a charge of breaking into a house at Kingston-upon-Soar. He was tried at the October sessions found guilty and sentenced to seven years' transportation. He was not well when he entered the prison. Everything was done for him that the surgeon ordered, both in respect to medicine, diet and attendance but he died on Thursday. Verdict: Natural death from natural causes, to wit, disease of the bowels.'*[194]

IV. THE FINAL DAYS IN THE LIFE OF CHRISTOPHER SWANN

Christopher Swann was at work until a few days before his death on the 24th December 1866, suffering from a diseased heart. One of his daughters, Sophia, was with him when he died at his residence in Sherwood, Nottingham. During the preceding months his health gradually deteriorated, although he had discharged his duties as a coroner up to this late period and it might be said '*that he died in harness*'. He had already selected a permanent deputy and it was his intention that this appointee would have commenced doing a good deal of the work.

Eleven days before his death he had presided at an adjourned inquiry relative to a '*high profile*' case of murder at Carlton (Table 8. p.59). It is possible that the anxiety of these proceedings together with other personal matters may have hastened his death. It seems that Swann, for some as yet unknown reason, was very much in debt and it is not clear why he should have died in such reduced circumstances. In the spring of 1865 he had written to the County Treasurer of the South Division requesting assistance with his financial situation. Although his letters do not appear to have survived the summary of the replies from Mr. Patchitt are available.[195]

In Memory of

Elizabeth Lois
the wife of
Christopher Swann
Coroner of the County
of Nottingham
Died March 20th 1861
aged 55 years
Also in
affectionate remembrance
of the above
Christopher Swann
who died December 24th 1866
aged 73 years
And of
Eliza Mary Swann
their eldest daughter
who died November 8th 1881
aged 48 years
Also Sophia
second daughter of the above
Christopher Swann
who died June 26th 1916
aged 71 years

Transcript of the inscription on the gravestone of Christopher Swann and some of his family in the Nottingham General Cemetery (grave 8453)

"*Dear Sir, Your letter reached me in London. I should be happy to oblige you but I really dare not begin a system of mixing public monies with private transactions.*
Yours truly, E. Patchitt, May 15 1865."

"*Dear Sir, I laid your note before the Committee today but I regret to state they thought they had not power to order any prepayment on account.*
Truly yours, E. Patchitt, Nottm. May 17 1865."

Christopher Swann was buried on the 29th December 1866 in the Nottingham General Cemetery and was laid to rest with his wife who had died five years earlier. Later being reunited with his two unmarried daughters, Eliza Mary and Sophia.

From his obituary we read: '*During the thirty-eight years Mr. Swann filled the office, his duties were discharged in a satisfactory manner. The fact of his being a sound lawyer enabled him to deal with legal questions with ease and with difficult cases he frequently exhibited considerable acumen and intellectual grasp. Above all, however, he was distinguished for his urbanity and courteous bearing, characteristics which never left him, but were as manifest at the last inquiry he presided over as when he was first elected to the office.*'[196]

1. The suspected murder of Henry Raynor

Volunteer, Carlton (c.1903)

The inquest previously mentioned concerned the death of Henry Raynor and was held, by Swann, with a number of adjournments, during November and December 1866 at the Volunteer public house in Carlton.[197-201] It was a difficult inquest for it concerned the suspected murder of Henry Raynor by John and Mary Watson and there were many complicated circumstances and it became a very protracted inquiry that was not concluded until after Swann's death. At one point the proceedings became acrimonious when it appeared that a policeman was accusing the defence counsel of tampering with the evidence. The bickering continued and at one point an exasperated juryman remarked: '*What has this to do with Raynor's death?*' A preliminary hearing, in a magistrate's court had already taken place. During the inquest the police were accused by the defence that some of the evidence they had already submitted at this hearing was not repeated to the coroner's jury. In addition, statements made by other witnesses seemed to be at variance with their evidence previously given. Mr. Swann suggested that:' *If further evidence of this character was to be given, it should be merely confined to a correction of statements made before the magistrates.*' This less than satisfactory gathering of the evidence must have been to the advantage of the accused and was clearly sensed by the defence counsel when he remarked when challenging a point of evidence: '*It can be overruled when it gets to court – if ever the case gets there.*' Eventually the coroner suggested an adjournment as he said that Dr. Taylor, of London, would not be able to give his decision with regard to the bloodstains, found by the police, in less than a fortnight. He would expect that the completion of all the evidence would take place at another hearing on the 1st January 1867. Christopher Swann did not live to complete this inquiry.

The house in Carlton in which the murder was believed to have been committed[202]

Henry Raynor was buried in the General Cemetery on Thursday 22nd November 1866; it was an event that created a great deal of excitement in the town and the Nottingham Journal devoted a whole column to the proceedings; part of which is transcribed as follows:

'*The masses of people who as early as one o'clock had stationed themselves in Broad Street, opposite the deceased's residence and place of business, was a strong proof how easy a crowd may be drawn together in Nottingham. By two o'clock the part of the street reaching from his office to the end of Glasshouse Street was filled with persons evidently from the lower parts of the town. At the corner of Lenton Street also above Raynor's office, there was a dense mass, and probably 3000 persons assembled. A considerable portion of the crowd were women, knots of whom discussed the deceased man's character with a freedom of language rather astounding to those persons who are unfamiliar with the style of conversation prevalent in the locality of Millstone Lane. Others failing a more profitable occupation, gazed with a melancholy interest on the extraordinary signboard over the deceased's door. In the centre are the words "Bailiff's Office" and at each end are the following: "Bills of sale and other instruments carried into effect," "Rents or debts recovered by distraint."... The cortege, consisting of a hearse and two mourning coaches proceeded up Parliament Street and Wollaton Street and reached the Derby Road entrance to the General Cemetery about ten minutes past three o'clock. The crowd made their way through the gates into the cemetery with a triumphant rush ... Mr. W. Frisby, the cemetery chaplain, addressed a few words of consolation to the relations (consisting of the deceased's wife, his sister, brothers, brother-in-law and two clerks). .... After a suitable prayer had been offered, the coffin was borne to the grave in the presence of probably 5000 spectators. .... The coffin was a plain oaken one, the plate bearing the following inscription: Henry Raynor, died Nov. 17, 1866 aged 31 years.'*[203]

His headstone bears his name and that of his wife Ann who, in May 1868 had married George Wesson. Other members of the family were also buried in the same plot.

A few weeks later Christopher Swann followed Henry Raynor to his own grave in Nottingham's General Cemetery but it is somewhat ironical that on this occasion the columns of the local press were bereft of any notification of the event.

A report of the police investigation and inquest on the suspected murder of Henry Raynor has recently been published, in the Nottingham Family History Society Journal, by one of his descendants and makes fascinating reading.[204]

In Memory of

HENRY RAYNOR
Died Novr. 17th 1866 aged 31 years
WILLIAM OLDHAM
Died Decr. 10th 1870 aged 43 years
ERNEST WESSON
Died Feby. 2nd 1875 aged 3 months
HAROLD SPENCER
Died Aug. 3rd 1889 aged 5 years
and of
ANN WESSON
Died May 2nd 1893 aged 60 years

Transcript of the inscription on the gravestone of Henry Raynor and some of his family in the Nottingham General Cemetery (grave 7673)

At the adjourned inquest on the 1st January 1867, William Newton, one of the Coroners for the county, presided. He was acting in a temporary capacity until a successor to Christopher Swann was elected. At the outset of this inquiry Newton explained to the jury that the death of Mr. Swann had left a somewhat complicated '*state of affairs*'. He told them that as the law stands their duties were at an end. According to the law, an inquest of death can be taken by a coroner '*super visum corporis'* only, and if there be no view of the body the inquisition is void. Although the statute '*de officio coronatoris'* does not say expressly that the coroner shall take his inquest on view of the dead body and that an inquest otherwise taken by him shall be void. Yet it is clearly laid down in the reference books that a coroner has no authority to take an inquest of death without a view of the body and that if he does the inquisition is void, and would therefore be regarded as an extra-judicial proceeding. It is true that the jury had viewed the body but not in the presence of the current coroner. The only way to resolve the situation would be to order the body to be disinterred and again swear the jury. The coroner in the face of no new evidence was not prepared to do this, as it would be very painful to the feelings of the relatives of the deceased. The jury were dismissed and no verdict was given.[205]

Nevertheless, the two suspects, John and Mary Watson, were sent for trial at the 1867 Lent Assizes but were discharged for lack of substantial forensic evidence.

V. THE SUCCESSOR TO CHRISTOPHER SWANN

There were two candidates for the vacancy; it seems to have been endemic in the election of coroners that complications would arise and the electors for this vacancy were not disappointed. The two contenders were Frederick William Parsons and David William Heath. At eight o'clock on the morning of Monday 4th February 1867 the poll was announced by the High Sheriff and took place at two centres namely County Hall and the Riding School. Initially a show of hands at a meeting on the previous Friday appeared to be in favour of Mr. Parsons, but this more formal election reversed the decision. When the poll closed at four o'clock it was revealed that 448 freeholders had cast their votes and 437 were in favour of Mr. Heath whilst only 11 supported Mr. Parsons. The Under Sheriff then adjourned the court until Wednesday morning when the return would be officially ratified. It was announced at this meeting that for some inexplicable reason, after he had actually triumphed at the first show of hands, Mr. Parsons retired from the contest. Nevertheless it was incumbent on the Sheriff to still proceed with the election:

'*Gentlemen freeholders of the County of Nottingham - we are met here today to conclude the business upon which we entered last Friday, namely, that of executing her Majesty's writ for the election of a coroner for the Nottingham District and Division of the County of Nottingham. On that day two gentlemen were proposed and nominated to fill the office and upon a show of hands being taken the majority of the freeholders present decided in favour of Mr. Frederick William Parsons. A poll was thereupon demanded on behalf of the other gentleman, Mr. David William Heath, and the court was adjourned until Monday for the purpose of taking the poll. On the evening of the day of nomination, the Sheriff received a notice from Mr. Parsons of his retirement from the contest. Now, I offer no opinion, gentlemen, as to whether, at this stage of the proceedings, it was competent for Mr. Parsons to retire. Neither was it competent for the Sheriff to dispense with the poll that he had granted as by so doing he would have been depriving the freeholders of the exercise of their constitutional privilege of voting. I may observe that the right of electing a coroner is, by the law of this country, vested in the freeholders of the county at large, resident within the district and no private arrangement or understanding between candidates or persons can in any manner take away or deprive the freeholders of that right. It was not competent for the Sheriff without such poll to return Mr. Heath – the only candidate remaining or willing to perform the duties of the office – because if the Sheriff had done so he would have returned a gentleman against whom a majority of freeholders had decided.*'[206]

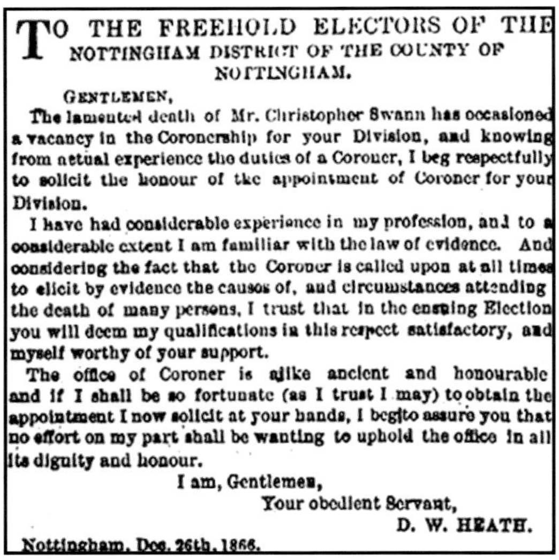

TO THE FREEHOLD ELECTORS OF THE NOTTINGHAM DISTRICT OF THE COUNTY OF NOTTINGHAM.

GENTLEMEN,

The lamented death of Mr. Christopher Swann has occasioned a vacancy in the Coronership for your Division, and knowing from actual experience the duties of a Coroner, I beg respectfully to solicit the honour of the appointment of Coroner for your Division.

I have had considerable experience in my profession, and to a considerable extent I am familiar with the law of evidence. And considering the fact that the Coroner is called upon at all times to elicit by evidence the causes of, and circumstances attending the death of many persons, I trust that in the ensuing Election you will deem my qualifications in this respect satisfactory, and myself worthy of your support.

The office of Coroner is alike ancient and honourable and if I shall be so fortunate (as I trust I may) to obtain the appointment I now solicit at your hands, I beg to assure you that no effort on my part shall be wanting to uphold the office in all its dignity and honour.

I am, Gentlemen,
Your obedient Servant,
D. W. HEATH.

Nottingham, Dec. 26th, 1866.

Notice inserted in the local press by David William Heath requesting the support of the freeholders of the County, in the forthcoming election, for a successor to Christopher Swann

So in what must be termed *a non-election* David William Heath was declared the Coroner for the Nottingham District and Division of the County of Nottingham to succeed Christopher Swann and so another era began. At one time there was speculation that John Howard Swann, the youngest son of Christopher Swann, may have had an interest in succeeding his father but he later denied this was so. In fact he was active in canvassing for Mr. Parsons.

VI. DISCUSSION ARISING FROM THE TEXT

1. Attempts by the judiciary to restrict the number of inquests taken

An Act of Parliament, published in 1752, made provision for coroners to receive fees and travelling expenses. The main objective of this Statute was that hopefully, it provided an incentive for inquests to be held in all cases of sudden death and not as previously, confined to '*persons slain*'. Unfortunately, payment of these fees was dependent on the approval of the justices at the Quarter Sessions and it was the misguided zeal for economy on the part of these gentlemen that severely impeded progress towards an effective medico-legal system in this country [207] Yet, it was not until the end of the eighteenth century that substantial obstruction to the work of coroners became apparent.

During his early years in office Coroner Swann was subject to these restrictions and as we have seen (Section I.4) he often complained bitterly about the attitudes of the justices, especially in their attempts to interfere with his decision to hold inquests. He was adamant that they were facilitating and indeed inviting the concealment of murder, particularly in children. Even more difficult to understand were the views of the higher courts in defending the rights of the justices to impede the work of coroners. It is known that the restrictions placed on coroners varied from county to county and it is not clear as to the extent that the fees due to Swann were withheld because they believed a particular inquest should not have taken place. The justices also attempted to embarrass coroners by reducing travelling expenses. These payments had not been changed since they were first instigated in 1752 and their value in the nineteenth century was now eroded by inflation. Furthermore, in 1858 the justices in Nottinghamshire, in order to limit mileage claims, created the position of a third coroner so increasing the number of districts from two to three.

An attempt was made to improve the medico-legal system in 1836 when two pieces of legislation came on to the statute books. For the first time, it was possible to pay medical witnesses at inquests, although as we have seen, the justices sometimes refused payments for technical reasons in the interpretation of the Act. Secondly, the Births and Deaths Registration Act of 1836 provided for the registration of every death in the country. The registration of burials for the previous three centuries had been under the aegis of the ecclesiastical authorities who administered it with lamentable inefficiency. The new Act ensured that no dead body could be buried without a certificate from a registrar or a coroner's order. It is generally supposed that it led to many more cases of sudden death being reported to the coroner. From the records of Coroner Swann, in the years immediately after 1837, this increase in reported deaths was not particularly dramatic rising by about 30% (Table 3). Another Act published in 1837 (1 Vict. c.68 s.1) provided for expenses of medical witnesses to be paid out of the county and not the parish rate and that the coroner must settle the claims of all parties at the end of the inquest. This frequently had the effect that coroners would only hold inquests if they felt certain that the justices would approve their claims for expenses which had been paid out of their own pockets.

In the 1850's newspaper editors began to take an interest in the fact that justices were unsympathetic towards vigilant coroners over the holding of inquests and thereby promoting secret murder - particularly of children. The highest incidence being in those counties where the justices had been most active; Nottinghamshire did not feature in the list. This does not mean that Coroner Swann did not have problems with the judiciary, he clearly did. It may well be that their reasons for interfering with the coroners were not entirely based on economic grounds, for they also bitterly resented the coroner's power of committal on inquisition which they regarded as an interference with their own courts.

The Registrar General was highly supportive of the coroners, for in his report for 1856 he considered it necessary that inquests should be held, not simply for the reason that crime should be detected but also that the number of crimes might be prevented. In that year there were 324 coroners in England and Wales, who held 21,801 inquests. The total charges amounted to £67, 000, averaging £3 1s. 6d. for each death These charges not only included the coroners' fees (£1 6s. 8d.) but also mileage (9d per mile reckoning one way from his usual place of abode to the body). They also took into account medical fees for evidence, autopsies and analysis, witnesses' expenses, constables' allowances and occasional payments to jurymen and for the rent of rooms. Of these inquests nearly 10,000 bodies died from diseases or in ways not ascertained to be violent and that 11,393 died violent deaths. There were 482 charges of murder, manslaughter and justifiable homicide; of these 265 persons were committed for trial of whom 109 were convicted and 16 hanged. Few countries recorded so low a proportion of murders as this, yet the instant that the provisions of the law were disregarded and inquests were not freely held homicidal eruptions broke out.[208]

In his report the Registrar General cited the poisonings in Essex, also the atrocities in Norfolk, which had resulted from the interference of the office of coroner and the serial poisonings of William Palmer in Staffordshire, who was eventually caught and hung. It was stated before a committee of the House of Commons in 1851, that the constabulary of Staffordshire was instructed not to furnish notices of deaths to coroners, except where crime was suspected. Under these regulations Palmer committed several murders. The writer then criticised the policy of magistrates in re-considering the evidence of each inquest and striking off coroners' fees when they considered them unnecessary. As previously mentioned, their aim was apparently to keep down the county rate but the £67,000 named as expenses in 1856 was only a small portion of the rates. The fees received by 324 coroners, personally amounted to only £29,068 being on average rather less than £90 each and yet out of this those coroners who had deputies or clerks had to pay them. Of all the judicial officers the coroner was paid on the lowest scale whilst his office was second to none in importance and its requirements were high.

It is clear that working under difficult circumstances over much of his period in office Christopher Swann resisted the justices' attempts to control his activities. But how many of his juries' verdicts of suffocation, over-dose of opiates or cases of poisoning that were pronounced as natural death were undetected felonious killings we shall never know. It was not until 1860, as a result of the Coroner's Act of that year, that some measure of independence from the justices was obtained. Although the judiciary still retained controls over coroners' expenses the adverse publicity that they received had an impact and there was little interference with the coroner and his inquests from that date. In 1889, long after Swann's death, the last link with the justices occurred when the administration of the Quarter Sessions was transferred to the County Councils.

2. Social conditions in Nottinghamshire

The reports of the inquests of Coroner Swann, published in the Nottingham press, make fascinating reading for they give accounts of the activities of working class witnesses and the conditions in which they lived at the time of an unfortunate death. Although we do not have sight of the original documents, the transcripts written by the press reporter were often published in great detail. Apart from the names and ages of the deceased they sometimes included details of family relationships. These would often include marital relationships and perhaps more personal details such as:

'*the bastard child of*' or '*that the deceased was quite an idiot with a fish's mouth which was always open*' or '*was a dumb idiot'* or '*was a notorious prostitute*' or '*was intoxicated at the time*' or '*the mother was a great drinker*' or '*the father was a black man*' etc.

In addition the occupations of the deceased and sometimes those of the witnesses were recorded and occasionally home addresses were in part listed.

It has been noted that one in three inquests were on children under the age of nine years and reference has been made to their poor social standing. One can perhaps surmise that the offspring of the poorer classes were often regarded as expendable. In the previous paragraphs the possible secret murder of children has been discussed. Opium-containing products were widely used for children primarily to induce sleep, particularly when working mothers left their progeny in the charge of unskilled baby-minders. It was well known that the margin of safety of these products, in the young, was very narrow and fatalities were inevitable in the hands of unskilled parents or grandparents. The onerous task for the coroner and his jury was to determine whether or not death had occurred from ignorance or was deliberate. The parents were invariably cleared of any misdemeanour, for instance:

'*Verdict: That the deceased has been poisoned by an overdose of laudanum being administered to her by her mother but there is not sufficient evidence to satisfy the jury that the mother wilfully intended to destroy the life of her child.*'

The editor of the Nottingham Journal was forthright in his condemnation of the practice of sedating children:

'*When so many instances have appeared in the public papers of children being brought to an untimely end by the improper use of narcotics, we cannot but express our strong surprise that so many mothers should still persist in dosing their infants with these sleeping potions. Numbers of females are in the constant habit of drenching their little ones with anodynes, 'Godfrey's Cordial', syrup of poppies, laudanum and other nostrums, to cause sleep in a way which Nature never intended. Many little innocents are by these means hurried out of existence and are made to sleep the sleep of death*!'

A brief reference should be made to burial clubs through which the lives of children were insured. These clubs were sometimes controlled by undertakers and publicans, who acted as treasurers, collecting the contributions from parents wishing to insure against funeral expenses. However, parents would often receive money over and above the cost of a funeral on the death of a child and this together with the obstruction by the justices to holding inquests, the temptation for infanticide for the sake of financial reward must have been great. The moral depravity and apathy to the fate of their children shown by the poor during this period of our history was appalling. Because a child was in a burial club, medical treatment for a sick child was often denied until near death for the sole reason of obtaining a medical certificate to facilitate registration and burial of the child's body. Obviously the abuse of this system was more prevalent in large cities but friendly societies also existed in villages and the urban districts and the same temptation to secretly dispose of children must have been there.

An examination of the statements made by witnesses sometimes includes a reference to the type of medical treatment or manipulation that had been attempted prior to death. We are also given a diagnosis of any concomitant illness or malady that may have been present in the deceased person. The primary aim of the medical men of the day was to rid the body of noxious substances and opening a vein to remove a quantity of blood was a very routine procedure. In addition the use of leeches applied to the skin served to attain a similar result. Purgatives and emetics were also commonly used to clear the stomach and the intestines of unwanted material. In order to save medical fees parents would often ask the local druggist to attend an ill child, sometimes with fatal results, as in the case where an unskilled practitioner forced a nutshell into the larynx of a child, which subsequently caused its death:

'*The jury is of the opinion that William Caunt* [the druggist] *is highly censurable for not giving the case to a regular medical man.*'

Parish officers were sometimes criticised by coroners' juries for their uncaring attitude towards those poor people who were dependent on them for the necessities of life. These reports often describe in graphic detail the living conditions of some of the most deprived persons in the community. Referring to an inquest in Bulwell in 1860 the Nottingham Journal noted that: '*The case is rather important and should be a warning to parish officers to be rather more vigilant in the performance of their duties.*' It concerned a woman aged 40 years whose death was occasioned for want of sufficient food and nourishment. Apparently the deceased was unmarried and had three illegitimate children. A friend had fetched the relieving officer to see her for she was ill and there was no food in the house. He had promised to send a conveyance for her to go into the Basford Union Workhouse but it failed to materialise. In the meanwhile the woman died. The jury returned a verdict:

'*That the deceased has died from natural causes, but that her death has been accelerated for want of necessary food and nourishment and that Mr. Harwood, the relieving officer, is highly censurable for neglecting to give proper relief.*'

Witnesses' statements taken from inquests held as a results of deaths in both the several workhouses in the county and the Lunatic Asylum often give us an insight into the organisation of these establishments. The names of other inmates present at the time and the identity of the officials and medical men were often recorded. This may well be a valuable source of information where other records have not survived.

In many of the inquests the lives of the poorer people in our society were documented in great detail. The value of this information can be the more appreciated because it is taken from the mouths of the ordinary working class individuals residing in our towns and villages in Nottinghamshire. Normally one would not expect that deaths from known diseases would feature at an inquest held by Christopher Swann but on a few occasions this did happen. During an outbreak of cholera at Radcliffe-on-Trent during the summer of 1849, Coroner Swann interviewed a nurse, Sarah Bell, who described in graphic detail the unsanitary conditions in which the people in Mount Pleasant were living at the time (page 50). Her description of one of the houses is repeated below:

'*There is a privy under one of the bedrooms and it projects into the house creating a very bad smell. There is a sough against the house door, which throws out a noxious stench. There are many other privies in the neighbourhood and a pigsty above the house, which smells very disagreeable.... I have never heard of any Sanitary Board being established in this village, nor have I seen any person inspecting the place for nuisances. I have not seen or known of any means being used to clean out the sewers, whitewash the houses or improve the state of the village.*'

Possibly the present-day residents of Mount Pleasant in Radcliffe-on-Trent may be somewhat surprised to learn about the past history of their road!

Elsewhere in 1849, an outbreak of cholera in Basford prompted one witness at an inquiry to describe the local area as being:

'*In a most filthy state and the area is poisoned by manure heaps, ash-pits, pigsty's and privies all open to the atmosphere.*'

Both these reports gave high priority to the smells in the area. At that time it was the mistaken belief that the spread of diseases such as cholera was through atmospheric pollution and several years had to pass before medical investigation was to show that a contaminated water supply was the prime culprit.

Other aspects of contemporary living conditions were often revealed at a coroner's inquest:

'*There are seven persons of their own family living in the house together with five or six lodgers who were generally navvies. The house consists of only four small rooms.*'

'*The way to the upper room is by means of a ladder which the unfortunate little girl attempted to ascend whilst her brothers and sisters were asleep...*'

The conditions in coal-mines were frequently cited, in some detail, in the witnesses' statements. Access to a mine, via the shaft, was before the invention and installation of the cage, a very primitive affair. It consisted of a free-dangling chain connected to a rope running over a pulley system operated by a steam engine. Accidents were common as men, boys, asses and coal were transported by this system. In order to reach the chain in the middle of the shaft a platform called a bridge-tree was pushed over the shaft. At the start of a shift the men and boys would cross this platform and attach themselves to the chain and prepare to be lowered into the mine. Unfortunately sometimes mishaps occurred with a fatal outcome:

'*Yesterday morning about six o'clock while it was still dark, though fires were burning around the pit bank, the deceased went along with about twenty others to the pit. Matthew Henson who had care of the bridge-tree, went to push it over the pit so that the men and boys might fasten themselves in the chains to go down the pit. Unfortunately, the deceased reached the pit shaft first and failed to notice that the bridge was not in place. He reached out with his arms to lay hold of the chain and he also put his foot out to step on to the non-existent bridge and he fell to his death into the mine.*'

3. To conclude

Whilst the primary purpose of the nineteenth century public house was to serve intoxicating refreshment many of these establishments, even in the villages, were able to accommodate other activities. For example, space was set aside where meetings were routinely held and it was also occasionally used for the sale of produce, land and houses etc. Also because of the lack of other facilities in a parish, coroners looked towards the local inn to provide a suitable venue in which to hold an inquest. In this event the deceased person was taken into these premises in order to be viewed by the jury. Indeed if a post-mortem was necessary, this would be performed where '*the body lay dead*'. I cannot find any evidence that a publican was remunerated for this service, although where the house of a private individual was used, invariably that of the parish constable, the occupant did, it appears, receive compensation.

Ninety five inquests out of every hundred took place in a local hostelry; the printed stationery assumed that this was a routine occurrence, for the deposition forms (an example is illustrated on page 14) were headed with the words:

at the house of ....
known by the sign of the.......

It was not until the early years of the twentieth century, due to the provision by the local authorities of permanent facilities for the reception of the unfortunate dead that the use of the public house was phased out.

I am sure that many of Nottinghamshire's present-day innkeepers will be most surprised to learn of these somewhat macabre happenings that took place, in former years, within their premises. They must be repulsed by the thought that at one time malodorous corpses, sometimes in a mangled condition, had occasionally been taken across the thresholds of public houses.

VII. MISCELLANY

1. Children of Christopher and Elizabeth Lois Swann

Francis Edward	1830-?
Christopher Marriott	1831-1906 (died in America)[a]
Eliza Mary	1833-1881
Sophia	1835-1916
Charlotte Lois	1837-44
Henry Kirke	1838-?
Alfred Hurst	1840-45
John Howard	1840-1917 (died in America)[a]
Fanny Victoria	1843-1924
Elizabeth Lois	1846-? (died in America)[a]

[a]Information taken from the Swann Family Records (Nottinghamshire Archives DD/1959/3/9) – deposited by Geoffrey Oldfield.

2. Nottinghamshire County Coroners for the Nottingham District

William Ellison	c.1778-1805
Thomas Wright	1805-1828
Christopher Swann	1828-1866
David William Heath	1867-1880
David Whittingham	1880-1921
Herbert Bradwell	1921-1948
Claude Aubrey Mack	1948-1981

Prior to 1858 two coroners were appointed in the county and by agreement one covered the southern parts (the one listed in the Table) the other the most northerly parishes. The Boroughs of Nottingham and Newark appointed their own coroners, the Borough of Retford whilst entitled to its own coroner appears never to have made an appointment. Also the Liberties of Scrooby and Southwell were privileged to have a coroner. In 1858 the county was divided into three districts, Nottingham, Newark and Retford each having its own coroner. The appointments in the Boroughs of Nottingham and Newark were not affected.

This division of the county into three districts continued until 1981 when the City of Nottingham was merged with the County of Nottinghamshire to form one coroner's district. At this time Claude Aubrey Mack, was the coroner for both the Nottingham and the Newark District and Henry John Thompson the coroner for the Retford District. After these two gentlemen retired from their respective offices Anthony Charles Graham Rothera, who had been the coroner for the City from 1952, was appointed to take up the new post for the whole of the county. He continued to serve in this capacity until 1983 when John Langham succeeded him to be followed, in 1988, by Peter Jenkin-Jones. The present-day coroner is Dr. Nigel Chapman who has held the position since August 1993.

3. References

1. R. Henslowe Wellington, The King's Coroner being the Practice and Procedure in his Judicial and Ministerial Capacities, Baillière, Tindall & Cox, London (1906).
2. J. Jervis, On the Office and Duties of Coroners: with Forms and Precedents. Seventh edition by F. J. Waldo, Sweet & Maxwell Ltd., Stevens & Sons Ltd., London (1927).
3. C. P. Dorries, Coroners' Courts: a Guide to Law and Practice, John Wiley & Sons, London (1999).
4. J. H. Turnbull, The Coroner's Verdict, The Criminal Lawyer, Vol. 91 (March 1999), p.3.
5. N.R. (16 May 1828), p.1.c-d & p.3.c.
6. N.R. (26 December 1828), p.3.d.
7. N.M. (6 November 1840), p.357.d-e.
8. N.M. (30 January 1836), p.38.b.
9. N.M. (20 February 1836), p.62.b-c.
10. DDH 169/80, Nottinghamshire Archives, Nottm.
11. N.M. (10 September 1836), p.291.d.
12. DDH 169/92, Nottinghamshire Archives, Nottm.
13. N.M. (15 November 1839), p.364.a.
14. N.R. (29 November 1839), p.6.c.
15. N.R. (26 April 1839), p.3.c.
16. DDH 169/58, Nottinghamshire Archives, Nottm.
17. DDH 169/81, Nottinghamshire Archives, Nottm.
18. DDM 104/14/3, Nottinghamshire Archives, Nottm.
19. DDH 169/134a, Nottinghamshire Archives, Nottm.
20. N.J. (22 January 1858), p.5.d.
21. N.M. (10 November 1832), p.360.c.
22. N.J. (19 August 1842), p.3.c-d.
23. N.R. (3 December 1858), p.3.e.
24. N.J. (28 July 1854), p.5.c.
25. N.R. (16 October 1863), p.5.c.
26. N.M. (29 August 1835), p.278.c.
27. N.D.E. (9 January 1906), p.8.d.
28. N.R. (26 September 1856), p.4.e & p.6.f.
29. N.R. (4 July 1856), p.4.e.
30. N.R. (27 November 1829), p.3.d.
31. N.J. (6 February 1864), p.2.d.
32. CA 1244, Nottinghamshire Archives, Nottm.
33. N.M. (23 April 1851), p.2.a-e.
34. N.M. (8 November 1834), p.354.a.
35. N.R. (15 August 1845), p.4.e.
36. N.R. (22 November 1844), p.5.d-e.
37. N.R. (17 November 1837), p.7.c.
38. N.J. (22 August 1862), p.5.b.
39. N.J. (29 December 1865), p.2.f.
40. N.M. (24 May 1828), p.3.c.
41. N.R. (30 May 1828), p.3.d.
42. F.B. Smith, The Peoples Health 1830 - 1910, Gregg Revivals (1993).
43. E. Lomax, The Uses and Abuses of Opiates in Nineteenth Century England, Bulletin of the History of Medicine, Vol. XLVII (1973), p.167.
44. V. Berridge, Opium and the Workers: 'Infant Doping' and 'Luxurious Use'. In: Opium and the People, Free Association Books Ltd., London (1999), p.97.
45. The Lancet (13 September 1862), p.299.
46. V. Berridge, The 1868 Pharmacy Act. In: Opium and the People, Free Association Books Ltd., London (1999), p.113
47. N.R. (16 August 1833), p.3.c.
48. N.R. (14 February 1840), p.6.c-d.
49. N.R. (28 July 1848), p.4.d.
50. N.M. (22 May 1846), p.301.e.
51. N.R. (2 November 1866), p.4.f.
52. N.R. (13 November 1835), p.3.e.
53. N.J. (19 June 1846), p.3.c.
54. N.R. (14 November 1828), p.3.d.
55. N.R. (26 December 1834), p.3.d.
56. N.J. (18 December 1863), p.4.g.
57. N.R. (26 October 1838), p.5.a.
58. N.M. (27 October 1838), p.341.e.
59. N.R. (22 April 1842), p.4.e.
60. N.R. (28 March 1845), p.6.f.
61. N.R. (20 October 1843), p.5.d.
62. N.M. (6 September 1850), p.4.e.
63. N.R. (12 April 1839), p.5.d.
64. N.R. (10 June 1842), p.8.d.
65. N.R. (1 February 1833), p.3.f.
66. N.R. (9 July 1847), p.4.d.
67. N.J. (28 April 1854), p.5.d.
68. N.M. (6 September 1850), p.4.e.
69. N.R. (1 September 1854), p.4.f.
70. N.M (22 September 1848), p.5.b.
71. N.M. (9 August 1834), p.253.d.
72. N.R. (10 October 1851), p.4.f.
73. N.R. (26 May 1843), p.4.e.
74. N.R. (22 June 1832), p.3.d.
75. N.R. (1 November 1844), p.3.c-d.
76. N.R. (22 April 1836), p.3.e.
77. N.R. (26 January 1864), p.2.c.
78. N.R. (29 April 1836), p.3.f.
79. N.R. (24 June 1864), p.5.e.
80. N.R. (13 October 1848), p.3.e.
81. N.R. (8 August 1834), p.3.e.
82. N.R. (1 April 1842), p.8.e.
83. N.R. (15 April 1842), p.8.d.
84. N.R. (19 March 1852), p.4.e.
85. N.R. (13 October 1837), p.3e.
86. N.R. (23 May 1845), p.3.f.
87. N.R. (6 June 1834), p.3.d.
88. N.R. (23 August 1833), p.3.e.
89. N.J. (9 December 1864), p.3.a.
90. N.J (19 March 1866), p.2.e.
91. N.R. (30 June 1837), p.3.f.
92. N.R. (24 August 1838), p.3.a.
93. N.R. (25 September 1846), p.8.e.
94. N.R. (4 April 1834), p.3.g.
95. N.R. (24 November 1854), p.4.c.
96. N.R. (22 December 1865), p.5.d.
97. NR. (15 May 1840), p.2.a-b.
98. N.R. (29 November 1850), p.5.a.
99. N.J. (25 June 1866), p.2.d.
100. N.R. (21 July 1843), p.6.e.
101. N.R. (6 June 1834), p.3.d.
102. N.J. (22 March 1839), p.3.c.
103. N.R. (6 May 1842), p.4.d.
104. N.R. (3 July 1835), p.3.e.
105. N.R. (27 June 1834), p.3.d.
106. N.R. (31 August 1838), p.5.a.
107. N.R. (28 October 1842), p.8.d.
108. N.R. (21 October 1831), p.3.c.
109. N.R. (9 January 1835), p.3.e.
110. N.R. (5 June 1835), p.3.f.
111. N.R. (4 April 1845), p.3.d.
112. N.R. (12 March 1841), p.6.d.
113. N.R (25 July 1828), p.3.d.
114. N.J. (3 April 1846), p.3.d.
115. N.R. (28 September 1849), p.4.f.
116. N.R. (23 November 1849), p.8.b.
117. N.R. (1 December 1837), p.7.d.
118. N.R. (1 March 1850), p.4.d.
119. N.R. (28 April 1854), p.4.e.
120. N.R. (14 April 1843), p.6.e.
121. N.M. (30 July 1847), p.8.d.
122. N.R. (27 June 1851), p.4.e.
123. N.R. (28 September 1838), p.4.c.
124. S. Best, Poor Chambers: The Dramatic Death of a Sneinton Man, Sneinton Magazine, No. 63 (Summer 1997), p.17.

125. N.J. (28 August 1863), p.6.b-c.
126. N.J. (4 September 1863), p.6.b. Quoting an article in the Illustrated London News.
127. N.J. (11 December 1866), p.2.f.
128. N.R. (1 October 1847), p.6.d-e.
129. N.R. (19 January 1849), p.8.d.
130. N.R. (17 November 1848), p.8.a-d.
131. N.R. (5 April 1861), p.8.a.
132. N.R. (4 May 1838), p.5.a.
133. N.R. (1 September 1837), p.3.c.
134. N.R. (10 May 1861), p.5.e.
135. N.R. (22 February 1833), p.3.d.
136. N.R. (20 September 1839), p.6.b-c.
137. N.R. (24 December 1847), p.4.f.
138. N.R. (7 April 1837), p.3.e-f
139. N.M. (8 April 1837), p.107.b-d. & p.108. a-b.
140. N.R. (14 April 1837), p.3.c.
141. N.R. (28 July 1837), p.2.b-f.
142. B. Holland, Across the Ocean Wide: An Index of those Persons Sentenced to Transportation in Nottinghamshire 1784-1867, Nottinghamshire Family History Society, Nottingham, Vol. 103 (1996).
143. C. Bateson, The Convict Ships, 1787-1868, A.H & A.W. Reed, London (1974).
144. N.R. (24 May 1844), p.5.b-c.
145. N.R. (31 May 1844), p.2.c-f. & p.3.a-f.
146. N.M. (2 August 1844), p.2.a-f.
147. N.R. (9 August 1844), p.4.a-e.
148. N.R. (28 March 1851), p.4.f-5.a.
149. N.M. (2 April 1851), p.2.a-b.
150. N.R. (11 April 1851), p.4.f.
151. N.M. (16 April 1851), p.6.c-d.
152. N.M. (23 April 1851), p.2.a-e.
153. A. Coleman, The Eastwood Poisoning. In: Eastwood through Bygone Ages, Eastwood Historical Society, (undated), p.123.
154. N.M. (25 July 1851), p.2.c-f & p.3.a-b & p.5.b-c.
155. N.M. (12 March 1852), p.4.e.
156. Personal Communication with Barry Holland who has obtained a copy of Sarah Barber's re-marriage certificate.
157. N.R. (7 January 1842), p.7.c-e. & p.8.a-d.
158. N.M. [Supplement] (18 March 1842), p.2.d-e. & p.3.a-b.
159. N.M. (4 March 1842), p.493.a.
160. N.R. (27 July 1842), p.2.a-e.
161. N.R. (10 September 1830), p.3.d-f.
162. N.J. (13 January 1864), p.2.d. & p.3.a.
163. N.R. (22 March 1833), p.3.d.
164. N.R. (22 March 1833), p.1.c.
165. N.R. (20 July 1849), p.6.b.
166. N.R. (27 July 1849), p.4.f.
167. N.M. (22 March 1850), p.5.d.
168. N.R. (3 May 1861), p.8.b.
169. N.R. (19 July 1861), p.8.b.
170. N.M. (29 December 1832), p.410.c-d.
171. N.J. (8 April 1852), p.5.d.
172. N.J. (9 February 1866), p.2.d.
173. N.R. (8 January 1858), p.4.e.
174. N.R. (18 July 1856), p.4.d.
175. N.M. (21 June 1844), p.99.e.
176. N.R. (28 April 1837), p.3.c.
177. N.J. (29 December 1865), p.2.f.
178. N.M. (28 January 1832), p.29.b.
179. N.R. (5 February 1841), p.3.d-e.
180. N.R. (16 September 1831), p.3.e.
181. N.R. (10 December 1852), p.4.f & p.5.a.
182. N.R. (11 March 1853), p.8.b-c.
183. N.R. (7 May 1830), p.3.d.
184. N.R. (25 July 1845), p.6.c.
185. N.R. (28 June 1850), p.6.f.
186. N.J. (4 August 1854), p.5.c.
187. N.R. (1 March 1844), p.6.d-e.
188. N.J. (7 April 1854), p.5.d.
189. N.R. (19 March 1858), p.4.e.
190. F. H. Jacob, History of the General Hospital, Nottingham, John Wright & Sons Ltd. London (1951).
191. N.R. (12 January 1838), p.3.d.
192. K. Brand, The Shire Hall and Old County Gaol Nottingham, Nottingham Civic Society (1992).
193. N.R. (11 January 1833), p.3.e.
194. N.R. (12 March 1852), p.4.d.
195. CT/18/2, Nottinghamshire Archives, Nottm.
196. N.J. (29 December 1865), p.2.d-e.
197. N.J. (21 November 1866), p.3.a-b.
198. N.J. (24 November 1866), p.3.a-c. & p.5.b-c.
199. N.J. (28 November 1866), p.3.b-d.
200. N.J. (30 November 1866), p.3.c-e.
201. N.J. (14 December 1865), p.4.a-c.
202. N.R. (7 December 1866), p.8.c-e.
203. N.J. (23 November 1865), p.3.b.
204. J. Granger, Shocking Murder at Carlton, Nottingham Family History Journal, Vol. 10 (July 2003).
205. N.J. (2 January 1867), p.3.e-f.
206. N.D.E. (7 February 1867), p.3.b.
207. J. D. J. Harvard, The Detection of Secret Homicide, Macmillan & Co. Ltd. London (1960).
208. N.J. (19 November 1853), p.8.b.

Abbreviations:

N.D.E. = Nottingham Daily Express
N.J. = Nottingham Journal
N.M. = Nottingham & Newark Mercury
N.R. = Nottingham Review

4. Source of illustrations

Illustrated London News

Children sitting in front of a fire (29.11.1862).28
Boy sitting in front of a steaming kettle (02.03.1844).30
Canal scene (19.02.1859).37
Exterior view of a coal mine (15.04.1843).39
Bottom of the shaft of a coal-pit (15.04.1843).41
Entrance to a coal-pit (01.02.1862).42
Power loom factory (18.05.1844).42
Three intoxicated men (18.11.1848).53
Gas-filled balloon (20.08.1859).54
Man attacking a woman (14.12.1861).74
Riot at an election meeting (08.07.1865).75
Congregation listening to a sermon (28.07.1855).78
A Coroner's inquest may have to take place (23.03.1844).102

Nottingham City Council Leisure & Community Services (Local Studies, Nottingham Central Library)

Broadside: Election of a Coroner (L34.19).vi
Broadside: Publicity by Christopher Swann (L34.19).2
Broadside: Publicity by Caractacus Shilton (L34.19).3
Line Illustration: Black Swan, Daybrook (57268).16
Line Illustration: Wheatsheaf, Cropwell Bishop (52999).21
Sketch: Trent Bridge Inn, West Bridgford (4680).22
Line Illustration: Crown & Woolpack, Sutton-in-Ashfield (77618).27
Photograph: Mason's Arms, Bulwell (25596).28
Photograph: Wheat Sheaf, Radford (25823).28
Line Illustration: Nag's Head, Kirkby-in-Ashfield (37779).33
Sketch: Lord Nelson, Burton Joyce (54868).35
Section of a 1884 Map: Fox & Crown, Holme Lane.38
Line Illustration: Ferry Inn, Wilford (4757).38
Section of a 1901 Map: Jolly Angler, Beeston.38
Line Illustration: White Hart, Lenton (1139).39,57
Line Illustration: Admiral Rodney, Wollaton (78138).39
Section of a 1882 Map: William IV, Carrington.43
Line Illustration: Waggon & Coals, Mansfield (3750).43
Line Illustration: Bull's Head, Mansfield (39941).44
Line Illustration: Windmill, Sneinton (21705).46
Line Illustration: Fox, Sneinton (44545).46
Line Illustration: Three Horse Shoes, East Leake (61748).47
Line Illustration: Admiral Rodney, Calverton (92734).48
Line Illustration: Red Heart, Ruddington (4270).49
Line Illustration: Brown Cow, Mansfield (74609).52
Line Illustration: Cross Keys, Arnold (91131).53
Engraving: Wollaton Hall (2413).56
Line Illustration: Gate Hangs Well, Brewhouse Yard (92757).56
Line Illustration: Trip to Jerusalem, Brewhouse Yard (1133).58
Line Illustration: Horse & Jockey, Bulwell (misc.202).58
Line Illustration: Fox & Crown, Basford (90343).60
Engraving: County Hall, Nottingham (56178).62
Broadside (part): Execution of William Saville (L34.8).64
Line Illustration: White Hart, Arnold (22738).76
Section of a 1835 Map: Workhouse, Gedling.80
Line Illustration: Wheatsheaf, Mansfield (39249).81
Engraving: County Lunatic Asylum, Sneinton (11485).82
Engraving: General Hospital, Nottingham (68221).83
Photograph: Volunteer, Carlton (61269).86

Private Sources

Line Illustration: Cranmer Arms, Aslockton[4].15
Line Illustration: Three Crowns, Bulwell[4].15
Line Illustration: Blue Bell, Sutton-in-Ashfield[4].21
Line Illustration: Anchor, Gunthorpe[4].22
Line Illustration: White Lion, Selston[4].26
Line Illustration: Red Lion, Hucknall Torkard[4].29
Line Illustration: Robin Hood & Little John, Lambley[1].29
Line Illustration: Pheasant, Radford[4].29, 69
Line Illustration: Nag's Head, East Leake[4].30
Line Illustration: White Lion, Lowdham[2].31
Line Illustration: Bridge Inn, Oxton[4].33
Line Illustration: Commercial Inn, Beeston[4].34
Line Illustration: Denman's Head, Sutton-in-Ashfield[4].34
Line Illustration: Plough Inn, Lowdham[3].36
Line Illustration: Cross Keys, Epperstone[4].39
Line Illustration: Royal Oak, Watnall[4].40
Line Illustration: Half Moon, Hucknall Torkard[4].41
Line Illustration: Victoria Hotel, Beeston[4].44
Line Illustration: Manver's Arms, Radcliffe-on-Trent[4].45, 49
Line Illustration: Salutation, Keyworth[4].46
Line Illustration: Bell Inn, Sutton-in-Ashfield[4].47
Line Illustration: Bull & Butcher, Selston[4].48
Line Illustration: Chesterfield Arms, Gedling[4].51
Line Illustration: Robin Hood & Little John, Arnold[4].54
Line Illustration: Railway Inn, Lowdham[4].57
Line Illustration: King William IV, Sneinton[4].74
Line Illustration: Magna Charta, Lowdham[4].75
Line Illustration: Crown & Anchor, Mansfield[4].76
Line Illustration: Pear Tree, Basford[4].79

Nottinghamshire Archives

Warrant summoning the Constable of Halam to select four men to appear as jurymen on a coroner's jury (DDM 105/14/3).13
Record listing the signatures of the jurors who appeared at a coroner's inquest at Screveton in 1898 (DDH/169/134a).14
An example of a form on which the coroner would record the statements made by witnesses at an inquest (CA 1244).19

Newspapers & Books

Advertisement: Dalby's Carminative (N.M. 24.11.1832).25
Illustration: Stagecoach (N.M. 28.07.1843).32
Illustration: Train (N.M. 19.05.1843).44
Plan: The house where the murder by Thomas Greensmith took place in Basford (N.M. 08.04.1837).61
Illustration: Sun Inn, Eastwood (F.S. Williams,The Midland Railway: Its Rise and Progress, (1876).64
Sketch: The house where John Jones murdered Mary Hallam (N.M. 07.01.1842).67
Plan: The room in which the body of Mary Hallam was found (N.R. 07.01.1842).67
Sketch: Portrait of John Jones (N.M. 18.03.1842).67
Advertisement: A memoir of Henry Shooter (N.R. 01.10.1830). 70
Sketch: The house in Carlton in which the murder of Henry Raynor was believed to have been committed (N.R. 07.12.1866).86
Notice: Election of a coroner as successor to Christopher Swann (N.D.E. 02.01.1867).88
Sketch: Coroner's inquest (N.J. 26.11.1881).Back Cover

Abbreviations: see footnote on page 97

Line illustrations of some of the public houses have been derived from photographs in a computer programme
[1] From a photograph supplied by Mr. R. Custance [2] From a photograph supplied by Mr. J.W. Taylor
[3] From a photograph supplied by Mr. J. R. Jeffery [4] Authors collection

5. Acknowledgements

I would like to thank the staff of the Local Studies Library, Nottingham Central Library for their cheerful co-operation over the period of my research and especially, Dorothy J. Ritchie, for her assistance in helping to select the illustrations from their collection. I also acknowledge the help and courtesy I received from the staff of the Nottinghamshire Archives. In addition I am most grateful to Barry Holland for allowing me to have sight of his database that he has compiled on coroner's inquests in Nottinghamshire. I also appreciate the expert help and guidance that has been cheerfully given by Dennis Apple towards solving my computer problems and in particular the design of the front cover. My thanks go to Suella Postles, Museum of Nottingham Life, for providing supporting information and allowing me to use a copy of the watercolour of the Gate Hangs Well public house. I am particularly grateful to my wife, Pauline, who has painstakingly spent many hours' proof reading the text and correcting my errors and making most valuable suggestions to improve this book.

6. Explanation of currency and measurement terms

Currency and approximate present-day equivalents

£ s. d. is used to denote pounds sterling, shillings and pence

Old Currency	New Currency
One pound	One pound
One shilling	Five pence (p.)
Six pence	2.5 pence (p.)

Measurements and approximate metric equivalents

One inch (in.) = 2.5 centimetres (cm.)
One foot (ft.) = 0.3 of a metre (m.)
One yard (yd.) = 0.9 of a metre (m.)

7. Index to local places, deceased persons and noteworthy individuals

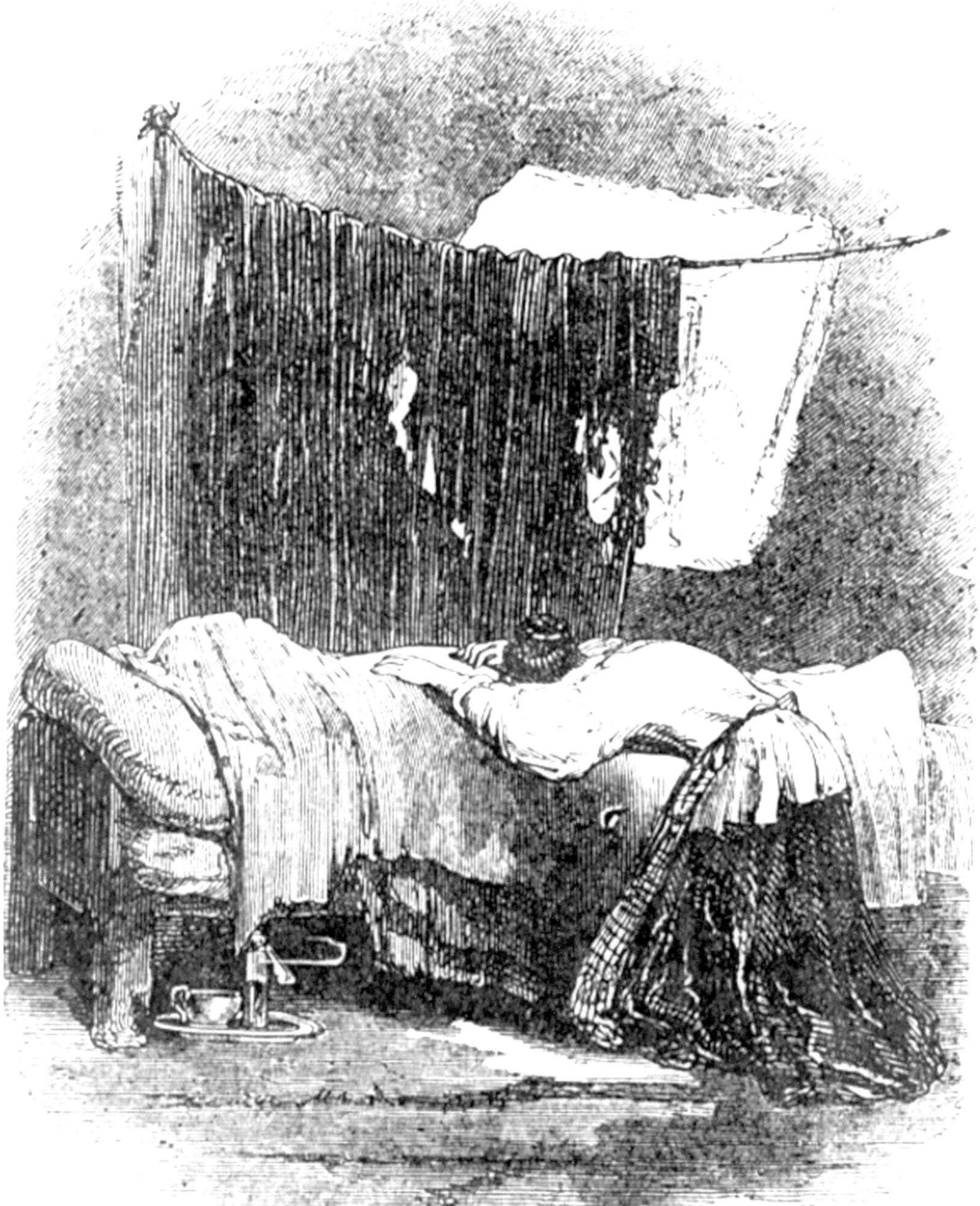

A coroner's inquest may have to take place . . . . (1844)